*Adventures in the Philosophy of Religion*

Books by Robert Leet Patterson

*Adventures in the Philosophy of Religion*
*The Role of History and Religion*
*A Philosophy of Religion*
*The Philosophy of William Ellery Channing*

# ADVENTURES
# IN THE PHILOSOPHY
# OF RELIGION

*Robert Leet Patterson*

AN EXPOSITION-UNIVERSITY BOOK

*Exposition Press*     *Hicksville, New York*

*To the memory of*
ALEXANDER RODNEY BOYCE

# Contents

*Adventures in the Philosophy of Religion*

# I

## *Philosophy, Religion, and Politics*

The title of this essay may, not improbably, produce in the minds of some who may read it an antithetical reaction. For, in the first place, it raises a host of problems so perplexing that to attempt to deal with them may appear to be overambitious. And, in the second place, although the study of history reveals that the interactions between these three forms of human activity have been manifold and vastly influential, it may with some plausibility be maintained that they have resulted from an illegitimate confusion of issues which should have been kept separate, and that, had they been kept separate, these problems would not have arisen, and that they may accordingly be dismissed as pseudo-problems.

Take, for instance, the relation between philosophy and religion. The former, we may be told, is the product of human reason whereas the latter reposes upon faith; so long as this distinction is clearly realized, no problems in regard to their interaction can arise. Here the name of Ritschl may well be invoked as that of the orthodox champion of this point of view. With more diffidence, perhaps, yet not without a certain plausibility, an analogous case can be made for a hard and fast distinction between religion and politics. Religion, it may be urged, is concerned with man's relation to another world, whereas politics is concerned with man's life in this world, or, again, that religion rightly concerns itself with man's life, his aspirations, and his destiny as an individual, whereas politics has to do always and only with groups and societies. And in the same spirit it may be contended

11

that although philosophy is a purely theoretical activity, politics is wholly practical; that the politician is concerned not with abstract ideas, but with facts, with measures to conciliate opposing movements, to satisfy conflicting demands, to devise measures productive of financial prosperity, to safeguard the military power of his country, and so forth.

The prior issue, that of the relation between philosophy and religion, is of supreme importance. It is an issue with which I have already dealt elsewhere to the best of my ability,[1] and were I now to discuss the subject in detail, I should merely repeat here what I have said there, thus enlarging unconscionably the present paper. Hence the reader will, I trust, be satisfied with the following of the conclusions there reached.

Reason, in my judgment, is the basic factor in religion as well as in philosophy. To admit this is not necessarily to disqualify the authority either of revelation or of mystical insight, but it is to admit that whatever authority these possess is imparted to them by reason. This does not mean that reason is divorced from emotion or volition but rather that it is fundamentally in harmony with both. The effort of the sound philosopher and of the wise religious man is in each case to envisage the universe as rational and to adjust himself to it—in other words to become at home in his world. Insofar as the thinker fails in his task, his thinking becomes alienated from religion, and insofar as the religionist fails in his task his religion becomes warped and malformed. Insofar as both succeed in fulfilling their functions, these functions tend to become identified, and insofar as this becomes accomplished we can say with Erigena that "the true philosophy is the true religion, and, conversely, the true religion is the true philosophy."[2]

It is the "true" philosophy, be it noted, that Erigena identifies with the "true" religion. If the universe be rational such identification is inevitable, for to apprehend ultimate reality as rational and to adjust onseself to it will be the work of the whole man, by the accomplishment of which he will attain intellectual and emotional satisfaction and volitional acquiescence. Intellectual and practical activity will then proceed hand in hand, and their perfect adjustment will constitute the ideal development of the whole personality. It is in this sense that philosophy and religion can be pronounced identical. To be rational, we may agree, is to be religious, and to be religious is to be rational.

Now it is clear that political activity is not, as I have represented it, wholly practical. Theoretical issues frequently obtrude themselves into practical considerations and claim the right to decide important questions. Moreover, it is plain that any political structure, no less than any theological structure, demands intellectual justification. Ethical, religious, and metaphysical conceptions play their part in politics; yet the field of politics is confined within this-worldly restrictions, and its theoretical content is thereby limited. Hence it can claim no more than to be a department of philosophy, and the topic which we are now to discuss can best be described as the relation between the philosophy of religion and the philosophy of politics.

With the twin problems of the origin of religion and the origin of the state in the sense of a political unit we need not now concern ourselves. When the anthropologist is silent it behooves the philosopher to hold his tongue. It suffices for us to take as our point of departure the generally acknowledged fact that man, so far back as our knowledge extends, has always been both a religious and a political being. Let us, accordingly, begin at the most primitive level known to us, that of the tribe. When we speak of a tribe we normally mean to refer to a group of people of the same race and language, inhabiting a roughly defined territory,[3] whose culture has not developed to a stage at which the term civilization can appropriately be applied to it, but which constitutes a society having some form of social and political organization. Some tribes are much more highly organized than others. Thus among some tribes of the American Indians the power of the chiefs was extremely limited, and the individual tribesman was sometimes prone to disregard it; whereas among the Pacific islanders a single chief was frequently endowed with absolute power, so that his tribe might be termed a primitive monarchy. In general, social organization is based upon custom; and custom, while it may not be unalterable, is regarded not as embodying tribal legislation, but rather as inhering in the nature of things, as having been imposed by the ancestors or by the divinites of the group. It is this which gives coherence to the group, and in accordance with it every individual is expected to regulate his activities.

The tribe was both a political and a religious unit. It was, so to speak, at once a state and a church. Sometimes the same individuals functioned both in religious and political capacities; elsewhere priests or medicine men constituted a distinct class, and chieftains another class. With the growth of civilization the primitive monarchy frequently continued to fill both a political and a religious role. Thus Israel and Moab had each its own king and its own God. With the growth of great empires, however, worldly power extended itself over religious diversity; conquered peoples were generally permitted to retain their own divinities, although worship of the gods of the conquering people, if not actually enforced, was at least expedient. But the rise of the great missionary religions transformed the situation; the same faiths passed from state to state and from kingdom to kingdom, and developed spiritual empires of their own.

That a spiritual unity thus established would give rise to a demand for political unity might seem a plausible supposition; yet, on second thoughts, it is clear that racial and local peculiarities and different historical backgrounds constituted an opposing influence. Moreover political rulers were loath to subordinate themselves to some central authority. In Europe, indeed, the effort was made, and a mighty effort it was, permanently to establish pope and emperor as coordinate spiritual and temporal authorities, an effort which finally collapsed in the outbreak of the Reformation.

This tremendous convulsion was followed by a proliferation of established churches in those states in which Protestantism had triumphed. Each church thus established regarded itself as the spiritual counterpart of the political organism to which it was attached. It is worth noting, however, that the relationship between church and state was not uniform. Thus in England today the official head of the Church is Queen Elizabeth II, whereas the official head of the Church of Scotland is the Lord Jesus

Christ. In the former case authority is theoretically imparted by the state; in the latter it is merely recognized. The spread of the spirit of toleration gradually permitted the growth of nonestablished churches. The American Constitution forbids the establishment of any Church of the United States; yet we must remember that, at the time when the Constitution was accepted, the Episcopal church was established in the state of Virginia and the Congregational church in the state of Massachusetts. Thomas Jefferson gave himself the credit of having brought about the speedy disestablishment of the former, but in Massachusetts the Congregational church was not completely disestablished until 1830. Yet, despite the fact that there is no established Church of the United States, the Supreme Court has declared the United States to be a Christian country, prayers are offered on the floor of Congress, and the President takes his oath of office in the name of God.

In Russia we find, in the light of history, what we may venture to term the normal relation between religion and politics completely reversed. A materialistic philosophy forms the basis of communism; hence, the investment of the leaders of the Communist party with dictatorial powers has produced for the first time since the Reign of Terror in France a government which is definitely and wholeheartedly antireligious. As far as they have dared, the Bolshevist leaders have discouraged the practice of religion, and the persecution which they endeavored to initiate would doubtless have been carried to an extreme were it not for the fear of violent reaction by the masses.

When the majority of a nation professes some religion, it is natural and almost inevitable that formal acknowledgment should be made on the part of the government; this is quite compatible with the toleration of a religious minority and the full recognition of the minority's political rights. Indeed, the absence of any such official acknowledgment would be difficult to account for unless the majority of the population professed no religion at all, or were fairly divided by their adherence to forms of religion so far opposed to each other as to render any joint cooperation between them impossible.

With all these considerations in mind, let us now survey in

broad outline the various forms of government that mankind has throughout its history adopted, and the relations in which they stood to the principles and ideals of philosophy and religion. Accordingly let us begin with the three forms of absolute government; first, that in which absolute power is placed in the hands of a single individual; second, that in which absolute power is placed in the hands of a relatively small group of individuals; and, third, that in which absolute power is placed in the hands of the majority of individuals.

## AUTOCRACY

The most frequent, as well as the most extreme, form of absolute government is the possession of unlimited authority by a single person. Usually the possession of such power, once acquired, is presumed to continue throughout the lifetime of its possessor; the phrase generally employed to designate government of this type is *absolute monarchy*. Of course the monarch conceivably may be overthrown by a rival potentate, but this would be in the nature of a political accident, having nothing to do with the theory of government. Again the monarch may become incapacitated by illness, physical or mental, in which case some arrangement must, perforce, be made. The heir apparent, if of proper age and ability, may with general approval and consent take over the reins of power, or, if no such personage be available, a leading counselor or general may function in the monarch's behalf. In normal conditions, however, the monarch will rule from accession to death. Yet absolute monarchy is not the only form of autocracy. Thus, the Romans made the world familiar with the notion of dictatorship—the entrustment, for a definite period, of a single individual with absolute power to enable him successfully to guide the country through a period of great peril. The same expedient has, of course, been tried elsewhere; not infrequently, indeed, an aspirant to power has proclaimed himself dictator and has, thereby, represented himself as the enjoyer of popular support.

In the case of an established monarchy in which son regularly succeeds father, the necessity of popular support is less blatantly obvious, yet none the less essential. It is true that as every master of a gang of slaves is in the position of a despot, so every despot is in the position of a master of slaves; indeed, his subjects frequently call themselves his slaves. Yet it is obvious that a single man cannot by his own physical power control a whole nation, or even a whole tribe. He must have subordinates upon whom he can rely if he is to coerce the majority of his subjects. Thus a conquering race may enable its chieftain to deal as he will with the conquered population. Yet the situation has often been reversed, and the people as a whole have thrown their weight behind a royal despot in his effort to eliminate or to subjugate a plurality of tyrannous nobles. One thinks in this connection of the Tudors, and of Louis XIV. Again a ruler may awaken popular support, and even enthusiastic loyalty, by his skill in dealing with military, financial, and social problems.

In this connection we should not forget the office of supreme judge assumed by many oriental rulers, together with the free access accorded to all who appealed for justice. In this connection one thinks, of course, of Solomon. An even more outstanding figure is the great Hindu emperor Aśoka, whose record in this, as in many other respects, is unsurpassed. And it is noteworthy that even such a monarch as Jahangir, many of whose acts were indeed reprehensible, habitually devoted much of his time to doing justice. Here we encounter the frank recognition of ethical claims on the part of despotism, which shows that a moral plea can be urged on behalf of this political institution.

In crossing the boundaries of ethics we enter the field of religion. We have already noted the sacredness of traditional custom to which is attributed a divine origin. What could be more natural than that a man who has been exalted above all others should be looked upon as the representative of the greatest of the national gods, or of one of the greatest? In Egypt, as we all know, the Pharaoh was regarded as an incarnate deity, as were some of the Sumerian monarchs and at a later period, some of the Roman emperors. The latest outstanding claimant to so elevated a position was the emperor of Japan, who, since his country's defeat, has modestly disavowed his divine status. Flattery and adulation, surely, played a great part in such deification of a ruler; and were he also a great conqueror, a reflection of his splendor doubtless illumined his followers. Yet, in addition to all this, there must have been a fundamental desire to establish, or to perpetuate, a union of the human and the divine. To attain this end, the development of the notion of incarnation must have presented itself as the easiest and most efficient intellectual instrument.

Yet, as one reflects upon the frequency with which this doctrine has appeared in history, and upon the importance attached to it, one can hardly fail to be astonished at the relatively little intellectual energy expended upon it by politicians as contrasted with theologians. The latter have developed rival interpretations of the doctrine, such as Modalistic Monarchianism, Nestorianism, and Monophysitism; contrasted with their intellectual activity, the attitude of the politicians seems extraordinarily lethargic. Are we justified in inferring that at the intellectual level of statesmanship the doctrine appeared mentally jejune, fit only for the uneducated masses? Perhaps we are. We may point out, however, without resorting to a doctrine as metaphysically complicated as that of divine incarnation, that the same end could be attained merely by proclaiming the king to be the human representative of the supreme God. So obvious a step has been frequently taken throughout the course of history not only in the ancient world, but also in such relatively recent times as the seventeenth and eighteenth centuries. The famous doctrine of the divine right of kings, while frankly acknowledging the complete humanity of the monarch, yet maintained that his right to succession, and his absolute authority from the moment that he ascended the throne reposed entirely upon divine sanction and was in no way dependent upon human consent.

Autocracy, it may be urged, wherever we find it is always the same thing. It is the possession of unlimited power by a single individual. Yet, as we have seen, this is too simple an answer. How did the individual acquire his power, and how does he maintain it? For as I have pointed out, no unaided individual could conceivably be equal to the task of controlling a host of other human beings, however he may excel over each of these human beings in strength and intelligence. If the master of a gang of slaves were to keep all his slaves chained up, they could not do any work. And if a monarch were able to imprison all his subjects, there would be none left to rule over. The autocrat requires support, if he is to be an autocrat.

Take, for instance, the rich men who built themselves castles in the reign of Stephen, and who turned them into "nests of devils and dens of thieves." Granted that they were all that the Chronicle calls them—"for cursaed," "for sworen," "for loren"—each robbing and ravaging at his pleasure, yet each was dependent upon the armed men who obeyed his orders and executed his commands. What he offered them was certainly nothing like a political constitution to which they might subscribe, and certainly nothing in the nature of a moral appeal. He offered them booty extracted from the captives they seized, and a sadistic satisfaction from the tortures they inflicted. He was, indeed, a local autocrat in the fullest sense of the word, yet his power rested upon the cooperation of his followers. Doubtless each man swore allegiance to him—a verbally unqualified allegiance— yet both parties knew that it rested upon implicit agreement.

The Roman dictator is, of course, the outstanding example of an autocrat whose power is explicitly imparted to him by an authority whom he recognizes and to whom he is responsible. What in his case was explicit is in the case of every autocrat at least implicit. Though a monarch be descended from a line of ancestors, the origin of which is lost in antiquity, and though traditional and unbroken custom confirm his legitimacy and unrestricted authority, yet the consent of his subjects—even though it be implicit, unquestioned, and unanimous consent—is the genuine foundation of his power. As the late Professor C. G. Field has well put it:

> Power, important as it is, is a derivative fact. The fundamental fact in politics, so far as we can talk of such a thing, is obedience, and it is from that power comes. The primary question to ask about any political situation is not who can crush whom? but who will obey whom?

Despite the fact that an autocrat must of necessity delegate power to others and rely upon the reports of others, if he be a person of superior ability, if he be a better general, a better organizer, a better judge of character than the average man, and if his ethical standards be high, it is clear that his government may not only be admirably conducted but may very well excel any other in dispatch of business and in efficiency of organization. But, alas, his mortality insures the termination of this happy state of affairs. Natural heredity provides no guarantee of the transmission of so desirable a character to his successor; rather does it assure us, though the dynasty be preserved, that a lack of continuity in moral and mental powers is inevitable. Nor has the wit of man devised any efficient substitute for hereditary succession. Herein lies the irredeemable weakness of autocracy. In certain circumstances and on certain occasions it may be pronounced by an impartial witness the best government possible; yet how rare those occasions and how complicated the association of circumstances! But when all else fails, when popular morality is extinguished, when intelligence is driven to the wall, when animosity of section to section, class to class, is rampant, autocracy will then present itself as the only alternative to anarchy.

## OLIGARCHY

We pass now to the consideration of that form of government which places unrestricted authority in the hands of a few, and since this is the literal meaning of the word *oligarchy*, we shall avail ourselves of it. Yet we must admit, I think, that the word has an evil sound; that it is suggestive of corruption and oppression, as habitually employed. Is not the same true, we may be asked, of the word *autocracy*? I, for one, could not reply in the affirmative without a qualification, for the notion of autocracy is a fairly simple one—absolute power, however acquired, reposing in the hands of a single individual. But under the heading of oligarchy we distinguish various forms of government by a few; we speak of plutocracy, timocracy, and aristocracy. These are different in their working, and even more in the ideas which inspire them.

## PLUTOCRACY

Plutocracy is, of course, government by the wealthy; in a pure plutocracy, it will not matter whether this wealth be inherited or acquired. What does matter is how much there is of it. Wealth, of course, need not consist only of bank accounts. Ownership of land which can be used for the raising of crops or for the rearing of cattle is likewise a great asset. The essential point is that the franchise be strictly limited to owners of property.

Unless the owners of property be animated by a nobler motive than the mere desire for wealth and its attendant benefits, and unless they can produce capable statesmen and generals, a pure plutocracy is a form of government which will be likely to fall of its own weight. At least the virtue of generosity should be sedulously cultivated if the disfranchised many are to be led to lend their support to the state. Yet, by manifesting a wise care for the general welfare, a plutocratic government may accomplish much. It would, perhaps, be unfair to describe the republic of Venice as a pure plutocracy, but that it was extremely plutocratic in its structure will scarcely be denied; its long history, resplendent with so many political, military, and financial successes, bears powerful witness to the potentialities of plutocratic government.

## TIMOCRACY

Timocracy is a word which we owe to Plato, and is used to indicate a state in which power is entrusted to the ablest, most courageous, wisest, most honored, and most honorable individuals. It is difficult to conceive how a satisfactory choice of such persons could be successfully accomplished. Doubtless the people as a whole must first be persuaded to support their government in designing and enforcing a strenuous and lengthy process of education, to which all the young are to be subjected, with a view to developing to the utmost their physical, moral, and intellectual potentialities. That a pure timocracy has ever existed is, to say the least, doubtful, although the ideal has not been without its influence.

As we are using the term *oligarchy* in its literal sense as meaning the government of the few, we are justified in treating aristocracy as a form of oligarchy, although, in so doing, we are running counter to the usage of Aristotle who contrasted aristocracy, as the government of the best, with oligarchy, which for him was an evil form of government practically equivalent to plutocracy. The government of the best! What more could we want? Ah, if only we knew how to bring it into being! There's the rub. Yet repeated failures should not blind us to the element of idealism which has usually been present in governments calling themselves aristocratic. An outlook at once ethical and esthetic is characteristic of the true aristocrat. Family pride is, indeed, the quality for which in common estimation he is most renowned, yet it is a pride which is rooted in the tradition of noble, courageous, generous, and trustworthy ancestors who have been faithful to their country and loyal to their supporters. Wealth and land, physical prowess, intelligence—all these are desirable assets, yet what is more essential than these is moral integrity. A ruling class thus endowed is the very backbone of the country to which it belongs.

## ARISTOCRACY

Are we, therefore, to conclude that a government in which all power is placed in the hands of a genuine aristocracy is preferable to any other? Before we assent to this suggestion let us look at the other side of the shield. We have seen that the greatest defect of autocracy consists in the inability to insure a succession of admirable autocrats. And the same defect is present in any aristocratic society. As Chaucer has well written, "Vyce may wel be heir to old richesse." And not only to old riches but also to old virtue and wisdom and courage and integrity may vice well be the heir; and not vice only, in the narrow meaning of the word, but also incompetence, stupidity, selfishness, disloyalty, and cowardice. A genuine aristocrat must be an all-round man. Hence, in manifold ways an aspirant to this role may fail not merely to attain to mediocrity, but also to avoid falling far below it. A man of good birth may easily acquire the bearing, manner, and accent indicative of his status, and yet, when put to the proof, may reveal himself as inferior to the average plebeian. Perhaps the greatest danger which confronts any aristocracy is the spiritual defection of its own members.

In a state in which an aristocracy enjoys not only social preeminence, but also political power, great caution must be exercised to prevent infiltration from unworthy sources. To make birth essential to membership in the ruling class is to adopt the extreme precaution, yet to do so is to forgo any advantage to be derived from the infusion of "new blood." A more moderate attitude would express itself by making admission dependent upon approval by all, or by the majority, of the upper class. And yet the numbers of such admissions must be narrowly restricted if the ruling class is to retain its traditional characteristics. Heredity is the permanent foundation of this form of government. A nobleman is subjected as a youth to the training which his forebears deem most efficacious, and if indeed it prove to be so, his future career will be all that they have hoped.

We cannot take leave of this topic, however, without turning attention to the development in the twelfth and thirteenth centuries in southern Europe of the ideal of the gentleman among troubadours and nobles. It was a movement which spread northward, and which finds its most impressive exposition in English in Chaucer's poem entitled "Gentilesse," and also in the following lines taken from the "Wife of Bath's Tale":

> But, for ye speken of swich gentilesse
> As is descended out of old richesse,
> That therefore sholden ye be gentil men,
> Swich arrogance is nat worth an hen,
> Looke who that is most vertous alway,
> Pryvee and apert, and moost entendeth ay
> To do the gentil dedes that he can
> Taak hym for the grettest gentil man
> Crist wole we clayme of hym oure gentilesse,
> Nat of oure eldres for hir old richesse.
> For thogh they yeve us al his heritage,

> For which we clayme to been of heigh parage,
> Yet may they nat biquethe, for no thyng,
> To noon of us hir vertuous lyvyng,
> That made hem gentil men ycalled be,
> And bad us folwen hem in swich degree.

Here we discover an exclusive emphasis upon character. How it is acquired does not concern us. Wealth and birth are to be despised only when upon them is grounded a claim to "gentilesse." Education and training, again, may be necessary preliminaries to the acquirement of character, yet they are preliminaries only. All that matters, be it attained how it may, is greatness of soul. Wherever it is found, in any group, in whatever circumstances, there is humanity's noblest product—the gentleman, or, his counterpart, the lady.

A state founded upon such an ideal and composed of such citizens would indeed be a democracy of aristocrats. Perhaps in the future it may appear on earth. Insofar as it has actually been approximated to, civilization has reached its highest level. Between the ideal thus envisaged and the concept of timocracy there is some degree of similarity, yet the latter is based upon activity and attaches more importance to practical efficacy.

Oligarchy, as we see now, may be either appreciative of, or indifferent to, moral values. In Communist countries, however, we encounter a form of government that is definitely antithetic to moral values—antithetic in the sense that it denies their reality. In each of these states we find a hierarchy based solely upon the possession of greater and greater degrees of power in the ascending levels until it culminates in a small group, or in a single dictator—such as Stalin—possessed of absolute power. Here we encounter what we may call the materialistic counterpart of aristocracy.

## PURE DEMOCRACY

A democratic government is a government which places unrestricted power in the hands of the majority. Hence, democracy in its purest form is to be seen in some of the ancient Greek city-states, or in some of the Swiss cantons, in which all issues are discussed and all decisions are taken in a public meeting with the entire population participating and the will of the majority being decisive. Thus, as the domain of the Roman republic expanded, every Roman citizen had to go to Rome to vote. Modern democracies have resorted to the device of electing delegates to represent their supporters in a congress or parliament, to express their views, and to advocate whatever measures their supporters approve. It is only in this indirect fashion that popular government can function in a state whose population is too large to form itself into a town meeting. Clearly, however, if it is to function with a respectable degree of efficiency, popular education must have reached such a level that the average voter will be able to form a fair notion of the issues with which he is to deal in this indirect way.

When the majority is possessed of unlimited power it is plain that they can impose upon the state whatever limitations may appear desirable. An outstanding instance of such a proceeding, as we have seen, would be the choice of a dictator to hold office, either for a definite period, or at the pleasure of the majority. In like manner the possession and the acquisition of private fortunes or the ownership of land may or may not be tolerated. And the same holds true of the freedom of a minority to express its feelings or to give utterance to its views. At present, however, we are concerned with the notion of a pure, absolute democracy which has subjected itself to no constitutional limitations, and of this all that we are entitled to say is that it will reign supreme, whatever be the will of the majority.

What is likely to be the attitude of such a state toward religion? Clearly it need not be openly hostile, as must that of a Marxian state theoretically committed to a materialistic philosophy. But will it not, must it not, be one of official indifference? Certain crimes no doubt will be punished, yet this can be justified in the public interest and on purely pragmatic grounds. In a state in which all men are politically equal, must it not be assumed that differences in education, culture, intelligence, and ethical outlook are irrelevant? Can the state take a more positive attitude without transforming itself into a limited democracy?

Suppose, however, that the majority of citizens prefer the same religion, or belong to the same sect of the same religion, and suppose also that they are extremely prejudiced and intolerant. If they wish to disfranchise or to banish all dissenters, on what grounds can the wish of the majority be opposed? Or, again, if the majority belong to the same race, and if they be moved by the desire for racial purity, what is to prevent them from driving out all aliens? Obviously nothing. So long as the majority puts no limitation upon its own action, its democratic purity remains untarnished.

## FORMS OF LIMITED GOVERNMENT

By the term *limited* I mean to indicate any form of government that does not place unrestricted power in the hands of a single individual, a relatively small group of individuals, or a majority of individuals. We are, of course, familiar with the phrase "a limited monarchy," which is habitually applied to any country in which the head of the state is entrusted at the utmost only with a restricted degree of power. I say "at the utmost" because the above description is habitually used with regard to Great Britain, a state wherein the monarch is wholly without any legal power and, accordingly, is said not to *rule*, but to *reign*. But the term will apply also to any government with a single individual permanently at its head in which the power of the majority, while indisputable, is restricted by constitutional limitations.

### LIMITED MONARCHY

In the ancient world, as we have seen, monarchy reposed upon a religious basis. The king was commonly regarded as the representative of a god, the descendant of a god, or even as a god incarnate. This did not necessarily mean, however, that his power was unlimited. There may have been priests who were also representatives of the gods, and whose wishes had to be considered. Again, custom that acquires a traditional authority from its immemorial antiquity may prescribe somewhat narrowly the precise function of the king.

As we survey the growth of parliamentary government through the centuries, we observe the power of the monarch becoming more and more restricted and the process of representation becoming more and more expanded. At first, parliament included only powerful nobles and ecclesiastics, then representatives of important cities and of the land-owning class were admitted; subsequently, as the franchise was bestowed upon all owners of a small amount of property, the number of representatives was augmented, and so the process continued until parliamentary government has become completely democratic.

The history of the English parliament acquaints us with the formation of an unwritten constitution through the passage of usage into custom. Thus the power of veto, which was last exercised by Queen Anne, through the lack of exercise by her successors was allowed to lapse, and is no longer a prerequisite of the monarch. Again, George I, to whom English was a foreign language, gave up attending meetings of the cabinet, with the result that the cabinet meets today without the royal presence.

The divesting of the monarch of legal powers has had, however, a very important consequence. So long as the king enjoyed and exercised such powers, and was thus directly involved in the process of government, he had to be prepared to encounter opposition as well as to receive support in his efforts to carry out his plans. But once he had left the arena, the situation was profoundly changed. The monarch is now very much in the position of head of the family: the object of trust, emotion, and reverence, destitute of legal power and yet possessed of enormous influence, one whose advice—the outcome of a lifetime of continuous experience—may be appealed to and often may be welcomed by political leaders of all parties. It is significant, moreover, that officers of the army, navy, air force, and other persons in public trust take their oath of allegiance, not to the constitution, but to the monarch. Personal loyalty is thus an impressive factor in the situation, and conceivably might exert a decisive influence in any crisis of domestic collapse.

The more one surveys the British monarchy, the most power-

ful and the most respected of its class, the more one is impressed
by the fact that it is the product of a long and historical growth
and the more one realizes the impossibility of producing a
political counterpart without a similar lengthy and historical
development. Before it could be come fully established there
must have been a succession of monarchs who, whatever their
personal abilities, were individuals of high moral principle and
firm loyalty to their people.

## REPUBLIC

The word *republic* has a long history, as has also the word
*commonwealth,* with the details of neither of which need we concern ourselves. As used in recent times it has been regarded as
applicable practically to any government which is not a hereditary
monarchy. Thus Poland, whose king was elected, was described
as a republic. On the other hand any and every democracy can lay
claim to the title. Indeed it would be fair to say that while every
democracy is a republic, not every republic is a democracy. For
the purpose of our present discussion I propose to treat the word
as applicable to any government in which absolute power is
placed in the hands of no single individual, nor of any relatively
small group of individuals, nor of the majority of individuals.[5]
In other words, it is a state in which power, whether enjoyed by
individual or by class, is limited.

Such uniformity of usage is clearly compatible with widely
differing structures of political power. All citizens, for example,
may enjoy the right to vote; on the other hand, the franchise may
be narrowly restricted. The highest officials, again, may be
elected by popular vote, or they may be chosen by a congress or
parliament or by local legislatures. The typical republic is an
amalgamation of classes, each of which is happy to make its
distinctive contribution to the common good. It is this spirit of
mutual cooperation which distinguishes a republic from a plutocracy or an aristocracy, on the one hand, and from a democracy
on the other. "No class, as such," wrote William Ellery Channing, "should bear rule among us. All conditions of society should

be represented in the government, and alike protected by it; nor can anything be expected but disgrace to the individual and the country from the success of any class in grasping at a monopoly of political power."[6]

## CONCLUSIONS

We have now looked at the principal forms of government, both absolute and limited. We have observed that it is essential for any form of autocracy that aspires to secure for itself a permanent status to associate itself with, and to base itself upon, some religious conception that may be appealed to in justification of the exaltation of a single individual to a position of supreme and unlimited power. We have seen also that a government of the few, which is not prepared to rest upon force alone, must justify its claim to power either by materialistic or by ethical considerations. Thus a plutocracy may urge that the wealthy few, by their control of trade, benefit the majority and mitigate their relative poverty. A timocracy, again, may insist that the men in power are actually the best fitted physically and mentally for the task of government, and that the state prospers under their rule as it could not conceivably prosper under that of the many. An aristocracy, needless to say, appeals frankly to moral and esthetic values, which it claims to hold in reverence and to exemplify, and, unless it be an exclusive aristocracy, it permits those to join it who share its ideals and give evidence of their fitness to do so. Indeed it may be urged that the aim of a genuine aristocracy is to produce, so far as may be, a democracy of aristocrats. And this is why it tends to pass beyond the form of oligarchy and to make its contribution to one or other of the two forms of limited government.

A pure democracy, however, as such makes no direct appeal either to religion or to ethical standards. The claim to power on the part of the majority rests upon the fact that it is the majority. Every man counts as one, not because he is a good man or an intelligent man or an able man, but merely because he is a man. The superiority of the many over the few is not qualitative, but numerical. Of course the majority may by its own initiative limit its power in any way it sees fit, but by doing so it ceases to be a pure democracy. There is nothing in the nature of a pure democracy which renders it directly antithetical to religious and ethical standards. Unlike communism, it is not antireligious but merely in its outlook irreligious. There is nothing in its governmental structure which involves or implies any recognition of religious or ethical values. It is this-worldly through and through. Its outlook is limited to the *status praesentis vitae*.

The formation of a limited government may conceivably result from the reconciliation of rival tendencies. Thus we can imagine that three parties composed of the landowners, the manufacturers, and the proletariat of a particular region might agree that a constitutional republic came nearest to satisfying their respective desires, despite the fact that the first group might have preferred an aristocracy, the second a plutocracy, and the third a pure democracy. Again, in a community in which the education of the average citizen is at an extremely low level, the majority may prefer to have the actual work of government carried on by a highly educated minority while yet retaining in its own hands the power of expressing an ultimate verdict of approval or disapproval. Nevertheless we may agree that when the majority consents to limitation with respect to its own power, this decision will most probably be due to the acceptance of some ideal. And here both ethical and religious considerations will predominate. I say both ethical and religious, for although I recognize that an individual may at once respond to ethical requirements and reject the claims of religion as such, yet I would urge that the sphere of ethics falls within that of religion, and that it is highly improbable that any society as a whole would concede that there is an ultimate distinction between them.

The first step in this general direction will be the recognition of ethical principles as the basis of legal requirements. That there is a fundamental difference or, rather, opposition between right and wrong (good and evil) is generally recognized the world over, both by civilized and uncivilized peoples, despite the fact

that there are important disagreements as to the status of particular actions and particular attitudes. Notwithstanding this general
agreement, however, there are pronounced differences of opinion
as to the nature of moral principles. Does society formulate them
and impose them upon its members? Or are moral obligations
imposed upon mankind by external reality. If so, how do we
become acquainted with them, and what is their origin? Some
have believed that moral laws are divine commands proceeding
from a sovereign Deity, that they are purely arbitrary in character, and that human knowledge of them is imparted by revelation. Others maintain that the relation of obligation is imposed
upon us by values which are rooted in the structure of the
universe.

This last view is the one which I have elsewhere defended,[7]
and the soundness of which I shall in our present discussion pre-
suppose. In the light of this the objective reality of both rights
and duties becomes clear. The performance of the latter entitles
one to the enjoyment of the former. The term *natural rights* is
indicative of the fact that certain rights belong to man as a
rational being in a rational universe, and that legislation can
neither create nor destroy them, but is bound to recognize them.

A full discussion of the various arguments for and against
this position and of the metaphysical background against which
they stand out would vastly exceed the limitations of our present
discussion. What I propose to do, therefore, is to present briefly
the view of a theologian and philosopher whose position I have
elsewhere[8] discussed at length, namely, that of William Ellery
Channing. There is a peculiar advantage in so doing, for despite
the fact that Channing was a convinced and enthusiastic theist,
an ardent Christian, and a firm believer in revelation, his theories
are presented in so wide a perspective that they will appeal with
approximately equal force to any axiological idealist, be he a
theist, a pantheist, or a pluralistic idealist.

There is, Channing tells us, one all-comprehensive right,
namely, the right of every man "to exercise his powers for the
promotion of his own and others' happiness and virtue."[9] It is a
right which is teleogically oriented; in other words, it is the right

to fulfill the purpose of his existence. As a theist Channing regards it as the gift of God, but as to the fundamental and all-inclusive nature of this right the nontheistic axiological idealist will surely agree with him. From this "great fundamental right of human nature," Channing tells us, "particular rights may easily be deduced."[10] He is content, however, with stating "a few of them"; perhaps it would be fair to say that he considered their inclusion within the great fundamental right to be self-evident. Of these particular rights he proceeds to mention eight. Every man has the right "to exercise and to invigorate his intellect," to "inquire into his duty, and to conform himself to what he learns of it," to "use the means given by God and sanctioned by virtue for bettering his condition," to "be respected according to his moral worth," to "be regarded as a member of the community to which he belongs, and to be protected by impartial laws," to "be exempted from coercion, stripes, and punishment as long as he respects the rights of others"; he has a "right to an equivalent for his labor" and a "right to sustain domestic relations, to discharge their duties, and to enjoy the happiness which flows from fidelity to them and other domestic relations."[11]

What, however, of the right to vote? To vote is to participate in sovereignty—it is not a right but a privilege properly bestowed upon those who possess intelligence and character which render them fit to exercise it. "Were the proper qualifications for it required, they would not exclude one class rather than another. Their aim would be to exclude the unworthy of all classes. A community is bound to provide for itself the best possible government, and this implies the obligation to withhold political power from all palpably disqualified by gross ignorance or by profligacy for comprehending or consulting the general welfare—who cannot exercise the sovereignty without injuring the commonwealth."[12] We should endeavor, nonetheless, to develop a public school system which will educate our people both intellectually and morally so as to render possible the universal extension of suffrage.

In the same spirit Channing commends a feature of the original constitution which has since been abolished, namely, the election of members of the Senate by the legislature of the various states. It is clearly a timocratic ideal which thus inspires him to commend a measure which raises that body above "popular passions." He denounced, however, the doctrine of "Instructions" according to which the Senator functions merely as an instrument for the execution of the wishes of the people who elected him. His duty is to devote a broader vision than the average citizen can possess to the interests of his country. All this is in accord with Channing's idea of the purpose of a constitution, an idea which he has clearly and forcefully stated. He writes:

> By democracy we understand that a people governs itself; and the primary, fundamental act required of a people is, that it shall lay such restraints on its own powers as will give the best security against their abuse. This is the highest purpose of a popular constitution. A constitution is not merely a machinery for ascertaining and expressing a people's will, but much more a provision for keeping that will within righteous bounds. It is the act of a people imposing limits on itself, setting guard on its own passions, and throwing obstructions in the way of legislation, so as to compel itself to pause, to deliberate, to hear all remonstrances, to weigh all rights and interests, before it acts. A constitution not formed on these principles must fail of its end.[13]

The state exists not to abrogate, but to secure human rights. Insofar as its authority impinges upon them, the end is their better preservation. Thus it forbids every man to be his own avenger in order, by an impartial legal system, to protect the lives of all men; it takes some of a man's property in the form of taxation in order the better to secure to him the remainder. To the great fundamental right corresponds the great fundamental duty—to exercise that right. They are the two sides of the same shield. Channing maintains:

> The individual is not made for the state so much as the state for the individual. A man is not created for political relations as his highest end, but for indefinite spiritual progress, and is placed in political relations as the means of his progress. The human soul is greater, more sacred, than the state, and must never be sacrificed to it. The human soul is to outlive all earthly

institutions. The distinction of nations is to pass away. Thrones, which have stood for ages, are to meet the doom pronounced upon all man's works. But the individual mind survives, and the obscurest subject, if true to God, will rise to a power never wielded by earthly potentates.[14]

It is obvious that Channing's philosophy of politics is closely integrated, and that it has been formed in the light of his philosophy of religion. That philosophy, as I have pointed out, has a theistic basis, a fact which is important to emphasize. Yet there is a further fact which is even more important to emphasize, and that is that the conception of the self as an immortal being destined to spiritual development in a life to come is in truth the ultimate basis of the entire theory. It is, indeed, also the basis upon which most theistic views repose, yet the same cannot be said of all philosophies of religion.

Consider, for example, the absolute idealism of Bradley and Bosanquet, or that of Professor Blanshard. By these thinkers the self is conceived to be finite in its duration and ultimately to become absorbed in an impersonal Absolute. By Lotze, again, although the Absolute is regarded as an infinite self, it is also believed to bring into existence all finite selves by dissociating them within its own being, and to keep them in existence only so long as it has need of them. And much the same is true of the status of the self in the philosophy of Sámkara. Yet it would be absurd to maintain that these eminent thinkers are not religious men, or that their systems are only disguised forms of naturalism. Rather we must frankly admit that there are differences of fundamental importance between different religious outlooks, and that the most significant of these concern the status assigned to the self.

I would call attention, however, to the interesting fact that the same evaluation of the self as enjoying ultimate and indestructible reality, and the same belief that the state is only a means and not an end can be found within the realm of non-theistic philosophy. Let me present as evidence two citations from the writings of McTaggart:

"Compared with worship of the state," he declares, "zoolatry is rational and dignified. A bull or a crocodile may not have great intrinsic value, but it has some, for it is a conscious being. The state has none. It would be as reasonable to worship a sewage pipe, which also possesses considerable value as a means."[15]

My second citation is also from McTaggart's *Studies in Hegelian Cosmology.*

> I have endeavoured to prove, in the first place, that we gain nothing by calling society an organism unless we are prepared to assert that it is the end of the individual composing it. And, in the second place, I have endeavoured to show that there is nothing in Hegel's metaphysical conclusions which entitles us to believe that our present society is, or ought to be, an end for its individual citizens. But we can go further, and say that the true lesson to be derived from the philosophy of Hegel is that earthly society can never be an adequate end for man. For Hegel has defined for us an absolute and ultimate ideal, and this not as a vain aspiration, but as an end to which all reality is moving. This ideal we can understand—dimly and imperfectly, no doubt, but still understand. And to any one who has entertained such an ideal, society, as it is, or as it can be made under conditions of time and imperfection, can only be external and mechanical. Each of us is more than the society which unites us, because there is in each of us the longing for a perfection which that society can never realise. The parts of a living body can find their end in that body, though it is imperfect and transitory. But a man can dream of perfection, and, having once done so, he will find no end short of perfection. Here he has no abiding city.[16]

McTaggart was no less a devoted idealist than was Bradley or Bosanquet or Lotze, or than is Professor Blanshard. Moreover all are agreed as to the vital importance of religion, and each has developed his own philosophy of religion. Nevertheless the divergence between the view held by McTaggart and the views expounded by his fellow-idealists is indeed a yawning chasm. If the self enjoy only a transitory existence, and if it be destined to become absorbed in an abiding reality whence it has emerged only to run its brief course, then, since the state normally persists throughout a longer period than is embraced in the life span of any individual citizen, and may endure throughout a multiplicity

of such life spans, it would be utterly absurd to assert that the
end for which the state exists is the welfare of the individual.
But if, on the other hand, the duration of the state, however
lengthy, is limited, whereas the individual lives forever and is
capable of spiritual progress toward an ultimate and eternal goal,
it is the contrary assertion which will be absurd. On the former
view it makes good sense to say that the individual exists for the
state; on the latter view, it is nonsense.

How do these two opposing views affect one's theory of the
type of government to be desired? If the state be a more lasting
and more inclusive and, therefore, a greater entity than the self,
the end of government will be to conserve the state, to maintain, and, if possible, to increase its territory, to augment its
financial prosperity, to strengthen its military power, at whatever
sacrifice to its inhabitants may be necessary. These considerations
do not definitely determine whether an absolute or a limited
form of government is to be preferred. Such a choice will clearly
depend upon a multiplicaty of considerations, but it is also clear
that no fundamental principle will determine the nature of the
choice.

What, however, of the other view? Whether with Channing
one holds that although the self had a beginning, it was created
to live forever, or with McTaggart, we believe it to be eternal,
we can surely agree with both in their common conviction that
no earthly society can be "an adequate end for man." Will not
this inevitably result in the conclusion that a limited government,
whether monarchical or republican, will alone be compatible
with our basic conviction? But perhaps just at this point an objection may be advanced by the orientalist. The majority of Hindu
philosophical schools, he may point out, were as convinced as
McTaggart of the everlasting existence of the self. No more than
he or Channing did they hold that the nation or the state could
be an ultimate end for man. Yet absolute monarchy was the form
of government universally prevalent throughout India. Did the
Hindu philosophers think mistakenly? Or were there not enough
of them to affect the thinking of the many?

In both suggestions there is doubtless some truth. Doubtless the caste system tended to stabilize and solidify popular thinking. Doubtless also the line between this-worldliness and other-worldliness was too sharply drawn. We must admit, I believe, that the Hindus did not draw the practical conclusions implicit in their own metaphysical and moral ideas. To show in detail how we should draw them from ours would exceed the limitations of this discussion. I can but urge that granted the soundness of the conviction of the indestructibility and the high destiny of the self, and granted the belief in the objectivity of values, a view such as that of Channing and McTaggart is more defensible than any other.

## NOTES

1. See *A Philosophy of Religion,* especially bk. 1, chap. 4, and bk. 2.
2. *Liber de Praedestione,* capit. 1.
3. Of course the tribe may wander from one habitat to another, or may suffer disruption. Cf. the eastern and western branches of the Cherokees or the two groups of Saxons, one of which remained on the continent whereas the other landed in Britain.
4. *Political Theory,* p. 78.
5. Whether a government under which the head of the state is elected for life should be called a monarchy or a republic is, I submit, a question not worth discussing.
6. *Works,* p. 41, col. 2.
7. See my book entitled *A Philosophy of Religion,* bk. 2, chaps. 6-8. I have there argued in defense of the realistic theory of universals, and have urged that universals fall into three classes composed respectively of values, disvalues, and those which I have called neutrals, and, moreover, that we are obliged to instantiate and to preserve, so far as we may, all instances of values, and to eliminate all instances of, and to prevent the instantiation of, disvalues. In short the position to which I am committed is that of axiological idealism.

8. See my book entitled *The Philosophy of William Ellery Channing*, chap. 4.

9. *Works*, p. 698. col. 1.

10. *Ibid.*, col. 2.

11. This statement no doubt has reference to the restrictions of slavery, the whole discussion in which it occurs being included in an essay on slavery.

12. See William Henry Channing's *Life of William Ellery Channing*, p. 581.

13. *Works*, p. 895, col. 2.

14. *Ibid.*, p. 176, col. 1.

15. See his essay entitled *The Individualism of Value in Philosophical Studies*, edited by Dr. S. V. Keeling, p. 109.

16. *Studies in Hegelian Cosmology*, pp. 192-93.

# II

## *The Philosophical Basis of Channing's Soteriology*

I begin my paper with the frank avowal, which will astonish no one, that I am not an Arian. Let me immediately subjoin to it, however, the equally frank avowal, which may amaze some, that were I definitely committed to a Christian theism, I should consider the Arian position with the utmost seriousness. I fully realize that such a confession may seem ridiculous, almost indecent, in the ears of my contemporaries. What! Betray an interest in, nay, a sympathy for a belief which today no one thinks tenable, and which both Trinitarians and Unitarians of every shade and stripe unanimously agree in repudiating! Let me in the first place point out, however, that the vast majority of those who join in this impressive commination service have never taken the pains thoroughly to acquaint themselves with what it is that they so unhesitatingly and emphatically condemn. In the second place, let me state that in this paper I shall not attempt a blanket defense of Arianism, but shall confine my attention to the thought of a single man, a philosopher and theologian of whom all Americans can be proud, in my own opinion—if in no one's else—one of the great thinkers of Christian history, namely, William Ellery Channing.

When I first began to study his system, deafened by the universal clamor, I assumed that Channing's Arianism had no other source than his reverence for the text of Scripture, and was something in the nature of a theological fossil. I was, therefore, ready enough to credit the common view that toward the end of his life, he had practically abandoned it. What, then, was my astonishment to discover that it reposed upon a foundation in great part philosophical in nature, and that it fitted so perfectly into his closely integrated system that it seemed incredible that he should ever have renounced it! And I was relieved to discover that no less a person than Ezra Styles Gannett seemed to share my opinion. It is this doctrine which I propose to discuss.

At the outset I wish to emphasize that as clear, direct, and manly as Channing's style is, there is an almost Hegelian subtlety in his thinking. We constantly find concepts which seemingly present themselves as thesis and antithesis—such pairs of concepts as those of authority and freedom, natural and supernatural, transcendence and immanence, reason and revelation—*aufgehoben* or sublated in a unity wherein they are seen to blend and to reinforce each other. Channing's thought is like a shield with concave and convex surfaces which we must repeatedly turn from side to side to grasp the whole design. Let us look at his treatment of the antitheses which I have just mentioned, beginning with authority *versus* freedom.

No man ever emphasized with more solemnity than Channing the absolute lordship of Christ, and one of his chief quarrels with the Trinitarians was that they seemed to him to qualify it.

> To whom am I to go for my knowledge of the Christian religion but to the Great Teacher, to the Son of God, to him in whom all the fulness of the Divinity dwelt? This is my great privilege as a Christian, that I may sit at the feet not of a human but divine Master; that I may repair to him in whom truth lived and spoke without a mixture of error; who was eminently the wisdom of God and the light of the world. And shall man dare to interpose between me and my heavenly guide and Saviour, and prescribe to me the articles of my Christian faith? . . . This is what shocks me in the creed-maker. He interposes himself between me and my Saviour. He dares not trust me alone with Jesus. He dares not leave me to the word of God. This I cannot endure. The nearest possible communication with the mind of Christ is my great privilege as a Christian. I must learn Christ's truth from Christ himself, as he speaks in the records of his life, and in the men whom he trained up and supernaturally prepared to be his witnesses to the world. On what ground, I ask, do the creed-makers demand assent to their articles as condition of church

membership or salvation? What has conferred on them infallibility? "Show me your proofs," I say to them, "of Christ speaking in you. Work some miracle. Utter some prophesy. Show me something divine in you, which other men do not possess. Is it possible that you are unaided men like myself, having no more right to interpret the New Testament than myself, and that you yet exalt your interpretations as infallible standards of truth, and the necessary conditions of salvation? Stand out of my path. I wish to go to the Master."[1]

Was there ever a more eloquent expression of commitment to the absolute authority of Christ? Yet turn the other side of the shield and you find Channing boasting, "as far as I am a Christian, I am free. My religion lays on me not one chain."[2] And what is it to be free? "I call that mind free," declares Channing, "which jealously guards its intellectual rights and powers, which calls no man master, which does not content itself with a passive or hereditary faith, which opens itself to light whencesoever it may come, which receives new truth as an angel from heaven, which, whilst consulting others, inquires still more of the oracle within, and uses instructions from abroad not to supersede but to quicken and exalt its own energies."[3]

How are we to deal with these seemingly contradictory assertions of unquestioning discipleship and of complete independence? The key to a reconciliation is Channing's conception of Christ as the supreme liberator, the champion of intellectual and spiritual freedom. From this it follows that to think for oneself, and impartially to seek truth wherever it may be found, is to follow Christ, and, conversely, that to follow Christ is to become intellectually free. Hence discipleship and liberty are one and the same thing. The authority of Christ is not that of master over slave, but that of physician, teacher, and friend of the soul. Channing remarks:

> Jesus is, indeed, sometimes spoken of as reigning in the future world, and sometimes imagination places him on a real and elevated throne. Strange that such conceptions can enter the minds of Christians. Jesus will indeed reign in heaven, and so he reigned on earth. He reigned in the fishing-boat, from which he taught; in the humble dwelling, where he gathered

round him listening and confiding disciples. His reign is not the vulgar dominion of this world. It is the empire of a great, god-like, disinterested being over minds capable of comprehending and loving him. In heaven, nothing like what we call government on earth can exist, for government here is founded in human weakness and guilt. The voice of command is never heard among the spirits of the just.[4]

In like manner the notions of the natural and the supernatural tend to fuse together in the conception of a rational universe, a universe, that is to say, in which nature is under the control of Mind and which is ordered in accordance with a divine purpose. Without going into his very interesting discussion of the rationality of the miraculous, it suffices, I think, for our present purpose merely to stress the fact that for Channing, to be a rationalist means to be a supernaturalist.

As the Creator of the universe, Channing's God is, of course, transcendent; yet he is in no sense an aloof Deity. But as in the case of Christ, Channing's attitude toward him may, to a superficial gaze, appear extraordinarily ambivalent. On the one hand we discover a tremendous emphasis upon the importance of obedience. "In all things else," writes Channing, "man may deceive themselves. Disordered nerves may give them strange sights, sounds and impressions. Texts of Scripture may come to them as from heaven. Their whole souls may be moved, and their confidence in God's favor be undoubting. But in all this there is no religion. The question is, Do they love God's commands, in which his character is fully expressed, and give up to him their habits and passions. Without this, ecstasy is a mockery. One surrender of desire to God's will is worth a thousand transports."[5]

This sounds rather like the Mohammedan conception of God the master and man the slave. But turn the shield once again, and what do we find? "We conceive," Channing announces, speaking on behalf of his coreligionists, "that Christians have leaned towards a very injurious view of the Supreme Being. They have too often felt as if he were raised, by his greatness and sovereignty, above the principles of morality, above those eternal laws of equity and rectitude to which all other beings are subjected."[6] How are these doubts to be reconciled with the insistence upon absolute obedience? The answer is that even as the gods of Plato's *Phaedrus* owe their divinity to their vision of the Forms, so Channing's God is God because of his reverence for and fidelity to moral standards which he has not himself created. Channing continues:

> We believe that in no being is the sense of right so strong, so omnipotent, as in God. We believe that his almighty power is entirely submitted to his perceptions of rectitude; and this is the ground of our piety. It is not because He is our Creator merely, but because he created us for good and holy purposes; it is not because his will is irresistible, but because his will is the perfection of virtue, that we pay him allegiance. We cannot bow before a being, however great and powerful, who governs tyrannically. We respect nothing but excellence, whether on earth or in heaven. We venerate not the loftiness of God's throne, but the equity and goodness in which it is established.[7]

Lastly, it is in Locke that Channing finds the ground for the reconciliation of the superficially antagonistic claims of reason and revelation. This is accomplished by discerning the reflection of each in the other; reason, in Locke's words, is "natural revelation"; "revelation is natural reason enlarged by a new set of discoveries communicated by God immediately, which reason vouches the truth of, by the testimony and proofs it gives that they come from God. So that he who takes away reason, to make way for revelation, puts out the light of both."[8]

There is, in my judgment, a genuine grandeur about this aspect of Locke's thought which has not been adequately appreciated; moreover, between Locke and Channing, on the one hand, and some of the Hegelians of the right, on the other—among whom I would particularly mention John Caird—I seem to discern a community of spirit which does not appear to me to have received sufficient recognition. What Channing does, in general, is to defend the Lockian point of view, and he has some things to say about those who depreciate human reason, which make good reading at the present day. I cannot, indeed, refrain from citing the following passage: "He who is compelled to defend his faith, in any particular, by the plea that human reason is so depraved through the fall as to be an inadequate judge of religion, and that God is honored by our reception of what shocks the intellect, seems to have no defense left against accumulated absurdities. According to these principles, the fanatic who exclaimed, 'I believe, because it is impossible,' had a fair title to canonization. Reason is too godlike a faculty to be insulted with impunity."[9]

The last sentence of the above quotation is significant. If Channing, so far as this issue is concerned, makes any advance upon Locke, it is in an emphasis upon the reason as a mystical faculty, and upon the exercise of it as a means of communion with God.

> Severed from God reason would lose its grandeur. In his infinity it has at once a source and a pledge of endless and unbounded improvement. God delights to communicate himself; and therefore his greatness, far from inspiring contempt for human reason, gives it a sacredness, and opens before it the most elevating hopes. The error of men is not that they exaggerate, but that they do not know or suspect the worth and dignity of their rational nature.[10]

So much I have judged it necessary to supply in the way of background to his soteriology by citations from Channing himself. But there are two further presuppositions which must be grasped, if his christology is to be understood. The first of these is his doctrine of "essential sameness," which is nothing other than what the medievals knew as the theory of univocal predication. Explicitly and with the greatest earnestness Channing insists upon it as a necessary prerequisite to any knowledge of God that is worth the having. He asserts:

> God's goodness, because infinite, does not cease to be goodness, or essentially differ from the same attribute in man; nor does justice change its nature, so that it cannot be understood, because it is seated in an unbounded mind. There have, indeed, been philosophers, "falsely so-called," who have argued, from the unlimited nature of God, that we cannot ascribe to him justice and other moral attributes in any proper or definite

sense of those words; and the inference is plain that all religion or worship, wanting an intelligible object, must be a misplaced and wasted offering. This doctrine from the infidel we reject with abhorrence; but something, not very different, too often reaches us from the mistaken Christian, who, to save his creed, shrouds the Creator in utter darkness. In opposition to both, we maintain that God's attributes are intelligible, and that we can conceive as truly of his goodness and justice as of these qual-ities in men. In fact, these qualities are essentially the same in God and man, though differing in degree, in purity, and in extent of operation. We know not and we cannot conceive of any other justice or goodness than we learn from our own nature; and if God have not these, He is altogether unknown to us as a moral being; He offers nothing for esteem or love to rest upon; the objection of the infidel is just, that worship is wasted: "We worship we know not what."[11]

The second presupposition, which follows from the first, is the presence of divine potentialities in human nature. All minds, as Channing is fond of saying, are "of one family."[12] "You cannot," he tells his hearers, "think too highly of the majesty of God. But let not this majesty sever him from you. Remember that his greatness is the infinity of attributes which you yourselves possess."[13] To him who continues to object that the doctrine of essential sameness ignores the bottomless gap which sunders the finite from the infinite, Channing has an answer which is of peculiar significance, for it reveals what is, perhas, his most fundamental conviction.

I affirm, and trust that I do not affirm too strongly, that there are traces of infinity in the human mind; and that, in this respect, it bears a likeness to God. The very conception of in-finity is the mark of a nature to which no limit can be pre-scribed. This thought, indeed, comes to us not so much from abroad as from our own souls. We ascribe this attribute to God, because we possess capacities and wants which only an un-bounded being can fill, and because we are conscious of a tendency in spiritual faculties to unlimited expansion. We be-lieve in the divine infinity through something congenial with it in our own breasts. I hope I speak plainly, and if not, I would ask those to whom I am obscure to pause before they con-demn. To me it seems that the soul, in all its higher actions, in original thought, in the creations of genius, in the soarings of imagination, in its love of beauty and grandeur, in its aspirations after a pure and unknown joy, and especially in its disinterestedness, in the spirit of self-sacrifice, and in enlightened devotion, has a character of infinity. There is often a depth in human love which may strictly be called unfathomable. There is sometimes a lofty strength in moral principle which all the power of the outward universe cannot overcome. There seems a might within which can more than balance the might without. There is, too, a piety which swells into a transport too vast for utterance, and into an immeasurable joy. I am speaking, indeed, of what is uncommon, but still of realities. We see, however, the tendency of the soul to the infinite in more familiar and ordinary forms. Take, for example, the delight which we find in the vast scenes of nature, in prospects which spread around us without limits, in the immensity of the heavens and the ocean, and especially in the rush and roar of mighty winds, waves, and torrents when, amidst our deep awe, a power within seems to respond to the omnipotence around us. The same principle is seen in the delight ministered to us by works of fiction or of imaginative art, in which our own nature is set before us in more than human beauty and power. In truth, the soul is always bursting its limits. It thirsts continually for wider knowledge. It rushes forward to untried happiness. It has deep wants, which nothing limited can appease. Its true element and end is an unbounded good. Thus, God's infinity has its image in the soul; and through the soul, much more than through the universe, we arrive at this conception of the Deity.[14]

It is against this background that Channing proceeds to develop his Arian christology. But before we watch him go to work, two anticipatory objections at once suggest themselves. In the first place, since God and man have so much in common, what need is there for any mediator between them? God and man are, indeed, so close that it would seem, as someone has put it, that "there is no room." And in the second place, if there must be a mediator, need we go beyond humanity itself, with its wondrous potentialities, to find one? To both these questions we shall find answers as Channing proceeds to develop his own position.

His theory rests ultimately, indeed, upon a value judgment. For Channing it is quite evident that in the character of Christ

we see the exemplification of divine perfection. "We believe,"
says Channing, speaking both for himself and his fellow Unitarians,

> that God dwelt in him, manifested himself through him, taught
> men by him, and communicated to him his spirit without measure. We believe that Jesus Christ was the most glorious display,
> expression, representative of God to mankind, so that in seeing
> and knowing him, we see and know the invisible Father; so that
> when Christ came, God visited the world and dwelt with men
> more conspicuously than at any former period. In Christ's words
> we hear God speaking; in his miracles we see God acting; in
> his character and life we see an unsullied image of God's purity
> and love. We believe, then, in the divinity of Christ, as this
> term is often and properly used.[15]

Probably these statements would be subscribed to today by
many conservative Unitarians. Indeed, we find the same thought
expressed in Whittier's poem entitled "Our Master," selections
from which constitute hymns frequently sung in Unitarian
churches. It is only fair, moreover, to remember that Channing
believed himself to have far better grounds for such a judgment
than, in the light of subsequent textual criticism, any informed
and intelligent man would lay claim to today, inasmuch as he
believed that the Four Gospels had actually been written by the
men whose names they bear, and, therefore, that they record the
actual observations of eye-witnesses. Even so, his judgment
would not elicit universal accord. It is here, I confess, that I find
it hardest to follow Channing, for I am one of those in whom
the impression produced by the accounts of the life and teachings
of the Man of Nazareth has not been such as to evoke unquestioning or unqualified admiration. I am quite prepared to admit
that this may be due to my own spiritual blindness—indeed I am
frequently so assured by people who account themselves better
qualified—but there you are. This, however, is by the way.
Channing feels quite sure of his ground, and confidently expects
us to concur in his estimate of Christ.

"I believe him," he announces, "to have been a more than
human being. In truth, all Christians so believe him. Those who

suppose him not to have existed before his birth do not regard him as a mere man, although so reproached. They always separate him by broad distinctions from other men. They consider him as enjoying a communion with God, and as having received gifts, endowments, aid, lights from him, granted to no other, and as having exhibited a spotless purity, which is the highest distinction of heaven. All admit, and joyfully admit, that Jesus Christ, by his greatness and goodness, throws all other human attainments into obscurity."[16]

This being the case, what led Channing to espouse the cause of the Arians? Why did he consider the issue between these and the Humanitarians of sufficient importance to throw his influence against the appointment of Andrews Norton, an eminent Unitarian but a Humanitarian, to a professorship in the Harvard Divinity School? What is his grievance with the Humanitarians? His grievance is that their position seems to him absolutely incredible, and that it carries with it implications which he esteems dishonoring both to the character of God and to that of Christ, and, in addition, that it is incompatible with the truth of one of his own most cherished convictions, that of the freedom of the will. For if Jesus did not exist before his birth as a man, the perfection which he exhibited throughout his life could not have been acquired by conscious effort, by genuine volition, by a real struggle. But where there is no struggle, there is no triumph; where there is no combat, there is no victory. Christ's perfection, then, was only a pseudo-perfection, imparted to him from without and not acquired by himself. He becomes a spiritual automaton. His life is no lesson for us who are involved in the actualities of moral combat; from it we can draw neither inspiration nor confidence nor hope. All the genuineness is gone out of it.

On the campus of Hamilton College there stands a class stone, erected at a period even more remote than that at which I inhabited a neighboring dormitory, and on it is engraved in Greek characters the class motto, NIKHN MOXOHTEON, *Victory must be fought for*. It is one which Channing would have enthusiastically echoed, and the thought which it expresses inspired his entire christology. This, I admit, I should have discovered from the perusal of his published writings, but as a matter of fact, it was not borne home to me until, among his unpublished papers, I came across a fragment of a sermon or essay in which it was set forth with such clarity that I could not fail to see it. Channing writes:

> Freedom, freedom is the condition and element of all greatness. Make the mind of Jesus a machine—i.e., suppose it under influences which it could not resist, suppose it to be visited with such continual instruction and suggestion from God as to render its own exertions needless—suppose it to have motives urged upon it by omnipotence, which it could not withstand, and though faultless, he would have no moral worth, no virtue, no greatness.
>
> Christ's peculiar powers, revelations, and connections with God, instead of causing, determining, and fixing his character, were on the contrary the effects, results, and recompenses of his character. Instead of making him pure, they were founded upon his purity. He was clothed with all his high office, because he was endued with high virtue. He won his glory by his goodness. In saying this, I say of Jesus what I conceive to be true of all beings in all worlds. . . . Christ was no exception to the universal principle of divine government. Nothing but moral goodness, the settled purpose of duty, manifested in an obedient life, can gain the approving love of God.[17]

Not only, in Channing's estimation, is the moral character of Christ thus vindicated, but also that of God. Unlike the God of Calvinism who "out of his mere good pleasure" saves a chosen few from:

". . . that immortal fry
Of almost everybody born to die,"

as Byron sarcastically puts it, Channing's God is not only merciful, but just, and accords to Jesus no unmerited favor. Christ's nearness to God is the result of spiritual likeness. "To this perfect rectitude of his will, his reason, and his life," asserts Channing, "he owed not only his mission on earth but his crown in heaven."[18]

From this it follows, if Channing be right, that in some previ-

ous life, or series of lives, Jesus must, through struggle, trial, and
triumph, arduously and painfully have attained that perfection
which he now fully exemplifies. Only upon this supposition does
his life become meaningful. But what has this all, we may ask,
to do with us? If Christ be a superhuman being, what signifies
his perfection to us who are mere men? It signifies a vast deal,
according to Channing. And it does so primarily not because of
his manhood, but because of his selfhood. For the principle of
essential sameness assures us that man and Christ are selves in
a completely univocal sense of the word.

> Thus all souls are one in nature, approach one another, and
> have grounds and bonds of communion with one another. I am
> not only one of the human race; I am one of the great intel-
> lectual family of God. There is no spirit so exalted with which
> I have not common thoughts and feelings. . . . No greatness,
> therefore, of a being separates me from him or makes him un-
> approachable by me. The mind of Jesus Christ, my hearer, and
> your mind are of one family; nor was there any thing in his
> of which you have not the principle, the capacity, the promise
> in yourself. This is the very impression which he intends to
> give. He never held himself up as an inimitable and unapproach-
> able being; but directly the reverse. He always spoke of him-
> self as having come to communicate himself to others. . . . We
> read, too, these remarkable words in his prayer for his dis-
> ciples, "I have given them the glory thou gavest me," and I am
> persuaded that there is not a glory, a virtue, a power, a joy,
> possessed by Jesus Christ, to which his disciples will not suc-
> cessively rise.[19]

Any man who sets before himself any other goal than this is
not, in Channing's eyes, a true Christian; for this is the magnifi-
cent end for which he was created. And our assurance that such
is the case reposes, as I have said, upon the principle of essential
sameness. Yet, after all, Christ did become man. For man is man
in virtue of the union of his soul with his body. And the soul of
Jesus was united to his body in precisely the same way as that of
every man; thus Jesus is "very man," as truly man as any man
could be, even though he was also more than man. What was
the reason for this union? There was no absolute necessity about

it. It was, if I may put it so, a matter of spiritual strategy. Christ *might* have appeared on earth in a superangelic form.

"I feel, indeed," declares Channing in a characteristic strain, "as if, with my present views of the heavenly world, I should not shrink before an archangel. But these views I owe to Christianity. They were unknown when Jesus appeared. And perhaps I deceive myself. Perhaps with an archangel's form I could not associate the idea of *fraternal* sympathy. But with Jesus, who was born at Bethlehem, I can form this association."[20] And it is because of this union with humanity that Channing can boast that in Christ our nature has been exalted to heaven.

And what of the death of Christ? What significance does Channing see in this event, about which christological doctrine has centered throughout the centuries? What is his answer to the Trinitarian who reproaches him for slighting it?

> To this I reply that I prize the cross and blood of Christ as highly as any Christian can. In view of that cross I desire ever to live; and of that blood, in the *spiritual sense,* I desire ever to drink. I hope, as truly as any Christian ever did or could, to be saved by the cross of Christ. But what do I mean by such language? Do I expect that the *wood* to which Christ was nailed is to save me? Do I expect that the *material* Blood which trickled from his wounds is to save me? Or do I expect this boon from his bodily agonies? No! by the cross and blood of Christ I mean nothing outward, nothing material. I mean the spirit, the character, the love of Jesus, which his death made manifest, and which are preeminently fitted to bind me to him, and to make me a partaker of his virtues. I mean his religion, which was sealed by his blood, and the spirit of which shone forth most gloriously from his cross. I mean the great principles for which he died, and which have for their sole end to purify human nature.[21]

And, if the Trinitarian then ask how he can hope for divine forgiveness, if no bloody ransom have been paid for his sins, in an outburst of inspired indignation Channing replies, "the essential and unbounded mercy of my Creator is the foundation of my hope, and a broader and surer the universe cannot give me."[22]

In this brief sketch of Channing's view I have called attention to the importance which he attaches to the free choice of a free will, and to the great stress he lays upon the intensity of the struggle involved in moral progress. This may have given the impression that he would be prepared to echo the Buddha's injunction, "Betake yourselves to no external refuge." I must, therefore, emphasize that Channing is not a Pelagian. He repeatedly asserts that we cannot hope successfully to combat temptation or to develop our moral characters without divine assistance; indeed, he extols Unitarianism as the religion of grace—grace "free, unbought, unmerited."[23] Nevertheless he insists that it is never a substitute for one's own initiative. We cannot expect to receive it, unless we seek it; it will be freely given, but we must cooperate with it. Hence it would be fair, in my opinion, to describe Channing as a semi-Pelagian.

Such, in broad outlines, is Channing's soteriology. Forgotten, except for an occasional scornful reference, as it is today, in the eyes, not only of Channing himself, but of the majority of his coreligionists, both at the period during which he wrote and for nearly half a century to come, it constituted the pure Gospel, the genuine Catholic faith of the ancient and undivided Church. It will, I think, be conceded that it is in the prayers of a religion that we come closest to what is vital in its theology. Years ago, when wandering in the bookshop at the Unitarian headquarters on Beacon Street, I came across an old prayer book, designed for family worship and entitled *The Altar at Home,* in which I found the following prayer to be said on the Feast of Christmas:

O holy and almighty God, Father of mercies, Father of our Lord Jesus Christ, the Son of thy love and eternal mercies, I adore and praise and glorify thy infinite and unspeakable love and wisdom, who hast sent thy Son from the bosom of felicities to take upon him our nature, and our misery, and our trials; and hast made the Son of God to become the son of man, that we might become the sons of God and partakers of the divine nature; since thou hast so exalted human nature, be pleased also to sanctify my person, that, by a conformity to the humility and laws and sufferings of my dearest Saviour, I may be united to his spirit, and be made all one with the most holy Jesus. Amen.

With respect to its philosophical basis Channing's soteriology appears to me immeasurably superior to the Athanasian. Of the latter it is, surely, true to say, as Channing said, that

> its leading feature is the doctrine of a God clothed with a body, and acting and speaking through a corporeal frame, of the Infinite Divinity dying on a cross; a doctrine which in earthliness reminds us of the mythology of the rudest pagans, and which a pious Jew, in the twilight of the Mosaic religion, would have shrunk from with horror.[24] In opposition to the doctrine of the two natures, divine and human, Channing declares, We believe in the unity of Jesus Christ. We believe that Jesus is one mind, one soul, one being, as truly one as we are, and equally distinct from God. We complain of the doctrine of the Trinity, that, not satisfied with making God three beings, it makes Jesus Christ two beings, and thus introduces infinite confusion into our conceptions of his character. . . .[25]
>
> One God, consisting of three persons or agents, is so strange a being, so unlike our own minds, and all others with whom one can hold intercourse, is so misty, so incongruous, so contradictory, that He cannot be apprehended with that distinctness and that feeling of reality which belong to the opposite system. Such a heterogeneous being, who is at the same moment one and many; who includes in his own nature the relations of Father and Son, or, in other words, is Father and Son to himself; who, in one of his persons, is at the same moment the Supreme God and a mortal man, omniscient and ignorant, almighty and impotent; such a being is certainly the most puzzling and distracting object ever presented to human thought.[26]

The Trinitarian's way of escape, of course, is behind the smoke-screen of analogous predication. No term, we are told, can be applied to God in the same sense in which it can be applied to anything else. God is not a person in the same sense in which a man is a person, nor a self in the same sense in which any finite being is a self. God's qualities are other than ours—not wholly dissimilar nor yet wholly similar, although no man can tell where the similarity ceases nor where the dissimilarity begins. Having conceded so much, we next learn that in God there is no distinction between quality and quality nor between quality

and substance, that he is a pure, undifferentiated unity; yet not
one, of course, in the same sense in which anything else is one,
nor a being in the same sense in which anything else is a being.
The orthodox may call this a masterly retreat, but to me it seems
very much like a rout. The whole doctrine of analogous predication impresses me, I confess, as a juggling with words, or, shall
I say, a running with the ontological hare and a hunting with
the metaphysical hounds. I cannot tarry to discuss it further, but
shall dismiss it with the observation that I consider that Channing
has successfully shown that from the point of view of theism, it
concedes everything that is worth defending. Channing's own
position is, obviously, an honest and thorough-going personalism,
whereas that of orthodoxy is neither a straight-forward monotheism nor polytheism nor pantheism, but a muddle of dogmatic
assertions tempered by contradictions. I do not see how any
personalist can hesitate which side to choose in the controversy.

It is clear, however, that, if Channing's fundamental value
judgment be unsound, his whole christology collapses. More
than any other form of Christianity, Unitarianism has centered
itself in Christ; hence, it is peculiarly sensitive to adverse criticisms connected with his person. Yet these are criticisms which
few of us feel like pressing. We owe too much to Jesus, we are
too responsive to the ancient tradition in which we were reared,
to feel at ease in so doing. We fear to be both presumptuous
and vulgar. Yet it is fair to say, I believe, that to many of us the
claim that Jesus was morally and spiritually perfect seems a
tremendous going beyond the evidence, and even difficult to
reconcile with some of the evidence that we have. Yet, if this
claim be rejected, the heart goes out of Channing's soteriology.
The historic basis for it is ruined. We can no longer trium-
phantly point to the figure of Christ as evidence indubitable that
moral perfection is attainable by beings like ourselves, since one
who shared our nature has already attained it. It would be futile
to deny that this is a great loss. Of orthodox Christianity we
can, I think, justly say with McTaggart that it is a religion which
men might honestly believe to be true, but which no man could
wish to be true unless he were devoid either of intelligence or of

humanity. But the Arianism of Channing is a noble religion, which we could all wish to be true.

Is there any consolation to be had, on the assumption that we have no alternative to rejecting it? I am inclined to think that there is. For, while for Channing, human, angelic, and seraphic souls share the potentiality of divine sonship, the entire animal world falls outside his purview, as outside that of the average Christian. In the orient, however, in the case of some of the philosophers of the Mahayana, and in the west in the case of McTaggart, and, if McTaggart be right, in that of Hegel, we encounter the view that all reality is composed of selves, and, moreover, that all selves without exception are destined to attain perfection. This is, indeed, a soteriological vision of such breadth and magnificence that it well nigh takes away our breath. If, however, the claims of panpsychism and personalism can be reconciled, as McTaggart thought, and as I venture to believe, it may be possible to show that this vision constitutes an insight into the very heart of reality.

In any case, there remains Channing's doctrine of the potential divinity of man, founded upon the principle of essential sameness. It is this doctrine which sunders him, on the one hand, from the pantheist or panentheist who sees in the finite self only an adjective of, or a transient differentiation within, the Absolute, and, on the other hand, from the naturalist who sees in life and consciousness only a kind of miasma arising from the cosmic soil. It was this doctrine which inspired his philanthropy, his attacks upon slavery, his defense of natural rights, and his support of the Founding Fathers' conception of a balanced government based upon a constitution which would provide an adequate protection against tyranny in all its forms, autocratic, oligarchic, or democratic. It is this doctrine which is today denounced by the neo-orthodox as the offspring of human pride, and by the social radicals as aristocratic. It is this doctrine which is the hated enemy of communism in all its forms; and the no less hated enemy of that materialistic proletarianism which, kindled by the torch of an inferiority complex and fanned by the winds of envy and hatred, is sweeping our own country like a forest

56 *Adventures in the Philosophy of Religion*

fire. As we look around the world, we find that it has few friends and many enemies. Yet its friends are friends worth having, for they are no time-servers; they do not climb on band-wagons to bask in the atmosphere of popular approval, nor do they fear the denunciation which too often takes the place of argument. And its enemies, too, are enemies worth having, for they are the enemies that any true doctrine and good cause ought to have.

That this doctrine can be vindicated, if not upon historical, at least upon metaphysical grounds, all personalists, I presume, would agree. Most theistic personalists, I opine, would defend it, as Channing defended it, by an appeal to the theory of essential sameness. Nontheistic personalists would undertake, no less heartily, to defend it in another way. I cannot stay to discuss this issue, although to me it is one of the most intriguing and most challenging of metaphysical issues. I shall, therefore, conclude by allowing Channing to state, with his own inimitable eloquence, what he thinks of human nature. His words are good to listen to, for the thought which they express comes like a breath of fresh air from a century when human hopes rose high, and when reason was as honored as today it is depreciated.

> I do and I must reverence human nature. Neither the sneers of a worldly scepticism nor the groans of a gloomy theology disturb my faith in its godlike powers and tendencies. I know how it is despised, how it has been oppressed, how civil and religious establishments have for ages conspired to crush it. I know its history. I shut my eyes on none of its weaknesses and crimes. I understand the proofs by which despotism demonstrates that man is a wild beast, in want of a master, and only safe in chains. But, injured, trampled on, and scorned as our nature is, I still turn to it with intense sympathy and strong hope. The signatures of its origin and end are impressed too deeply to be ever wholly effaced. I bless it for its kind affections, for its strong and tender love. I honor it for its struggles against oppression, for its growth and progress under the weight of so many chains and prejudices, for its achievements in science and art, and still more, for its examples of heroic and saintly virtue. These are marks of a divine origin and the pledges of a celestial inheritance; and I thank God that my own lot is bound up with that of the human race.[27]

## NOTES

1. *Works,* p. 486, cols. 1-2.
2. *Ibid.,* p. 208, col. 2.
3. *Ibid.,* p. 174, col. 2.
4. *Ibid.,* p. 361, col. 2.
5. *Ibid.,* p. 381, col. 1.
6. *Ibid.,* p. 376, col. 1.
7. *Ibid.,* p. 376, cols. 1, 2.
8. *Essay,* bk. 4, chap. 19, sec. 4.
9. *Works,* p. 399, col. 1.
10. *Ibid.,* p. 338, col. 1.
11. *Ibid.,* p. 464, col. 1.
12. *Ibid.,* p. 313, col. 1.
13. *Ibid.,* p. 297, col. 1.
14. *Ibid.,* p. 294, col. 2- p. 295, col. 1.
15. *Ibid.,* p. 402, col. 1.
16. *Ibid.,* p. 313, col. 2; p. 314, col. 1.
17. See R. L. Patterson's *The Philosophy of William Ellery Channing,* p. 165.
18. *Works,* p. 1008, col. 1.
19. *Ibid.,* p. 313, col. 2; p. 314, col. 1.
20. *Ibid.,* p. 994, col. 1.
21. *Ibid.,* p. 1011, col. 1.
22. *Ibid.,* p. 398, col. 1.
23. *Ibid.,* p. 401, col. 1.
24. *Ibid.,* p. 388, col. 1.
25. *Ibid.,* p. 3733, cols. 1-2.
26. *Ibid.,* p. 390, col. 1
27. *Ibid.,* p. 299, col. 1.

# III

## McTaggart's Conception
## of Love

The most impressive feature of McTaggart's philosophy is his conception of love together with his estimate of its value. In my judgment it is one of the most penetrating insights in the history of philosophy. To discuss it at any length, needless to say, is to lay oneself open to severe criticism, either on the ground of having yielded to a sentimental attraction or upon that of having displayed a crude and coarse lack of appreciation; nonetheless I shall herewith venture to state my own opinion with respect to it.

Love, according to McTaggart, is purely emotional. This does not mean that it can exercise no influence upon volition but only that it is to be sharply distinguished from it. In other words it is neither to be identified nor confused with benevolence. Again love is not to be confused with sympathy. "There are cases," writes McTaggart, "where men rejoiced in, and desired to promote, the ill-being of those whom they really loved. Such cases are probably rare, they are certainly evil, and perhaps they are always caused by influences which may be called morbid. But they do occur. And, whatever may be said of such exceptional cases, it is clear that benevolence and sympathy, even if they were never absent when love is present, are often present when love is absent."[1]

What, then, is love? "Love," declares McTaggart, "is a liking which is felt toward persons, and which is intense and passionate."[2] Does love hold among values "a supreme and unique position"? "It would hold such a position," answers McTaggart, if it were true that love is capable of being so good, that no possible goodness arising from knowledge, virtue, pleasure, or fullness of life could equal it. And it is this view, a view which has been held by many people, mystics and nonmystics—which I believe to be true. It seems to me that, when love reached or passed a certain point, it would be more good than any possible amount of knowledge, virtue, pleasure, or fullness of life could be. This does not, so far as I am concerned, spring from any belief that I have reached such a point. It is a conclusion which seems to me to follow from contemplating the nature of love, on the one hand, and of the other qualities on the other hand.[3]

This recognition of the status of love among other values is the fruit of a direct awareness which is self-evident, of an immediate apprehension which is ultimate. Here I find myself in complete agreement with McTaggart. Dr. Keeling, however, has called our attention to the fact that McTaggart arrived at this position by departing from his earlier view which we find set forth in his essay entitled "The Further Determination of the Absolute"[4] "Love," we there read, "is not only the highest thing in the universe, but the only thing. Nothing else has true reality, everything which has partial reality has it only as an imperfect form of the one perfection." Of this earlier view we find, I think, an echo in his contention that love "is more independent than any other emotion of the qualities of the substance toward which it is felt."[5]

I do not mean that love is not reached, in our present experience, by means of the qualities which the beloved has, or is believed to have. If B loves C and does not love D, it can often be explained by the fact that C possesses some quality which D does not possess. And in some of the cases where neither B nor anyone else can explain why he loves C and not D, there may be such an explanation, though it has not been discovered. What I mean is that, while the love may be *because* of those qualities, it is not in respect of them.[6]

The distinction in the last sentence between *because* of and in *respect* of is of fundamental importance in the present connection, yet it is also one which it is not easy to make clear to oneself. McTaggart endeavors to help us by further discussion. "Love and hatred," he tells us, "are varieties of liking and repugnance."[7] Moreover "approval and disapproval are distinguished from liking and repugnance by the fact that they are for qualities, or for substances in respect of their possession of these qualities, while liking and repugnance are for particular substances or wholes, though they may be *determined* by the qualities of the substances."[8]

To make his point clear McTaggart brings forward an instance of the approval of one man by another. Approval, he tells us, is always both in respect of and also because of a quality.

> But the quality in respect of which I approve of him may be different from the quality because of which I approve of him. I approve of Cromwell, let us say, in respect of his courage. But what causes my approval? Its immediate cause is my belief that he was courageous. If we state this in terms of Cromwell's qualities, the cause is that he has the quality of being believed by me to be courageous. My approval is then in respect of one quality, and is because of quite a different quality. For to be courageous, and to be believed by me to be courageous, are quite different qualities. Of course, my belief that he was courageous may be determined by the fact that he was courageous, and then this second fact—his courage—is the remote cause of my approval. But my approval is in respect of his courage directly, and without any intermediate stage.[9]

And, after some further remarks, McTaggart states that "my contention is that while love may be because of qualities, it is never in respect of qualities."[10]

In support of this contention McTaggart points to what he takes to be three characteristics of love, "as we find it in present experience. The first," he continues, "is that love is not necessarily proportional to the dignity or adequacy of the qualities which determine it. A trivial cause may determine the direction of intense love. It may be determined by birth in the same family, or by childhood in the same house. It may be determined by physical beauty, or by purely sexual desire. And yet it may be all that love can be."[11]

The second characteristic is to be found in our attitude in those cases in which we are unable to find any quality in the object of love which determines the love to arise. In such a case, if the emotion were other than love, we should condemn the emotion. For since we do not know what the cause is, we cannot know if the cause is adequate. And without an adequate cause, the emotion is to be condemned. But we do not condemn love because it is not known why it is C, and not D, whom B loves. No cause can be inadequate, if it produces such a result.[12]

The third characteristic becomes evident in those cases in which he discovers that a person, whom he has loved because he believed him to have a certain quality, has ceased to have it, or never had it at all. With other emotions, such a discovery would at once condemn the emotion, and in many cases, though not in all, would soon destroy it. Continued admiration or fear of anything because of some quality which it had ceased to possess, or which it had erroneously been believed to possess, would be admitted to be absurd, and would seldom last for long. But with love it is different. If love has once arisen, there is no reason why it ought to cease because the belief has ceased which was its cause. And this is true, however important the quality believed in may be. If a man whom I have come to love because I believed him virtuous or brave proves to be vicious or cowardly, this may make me miserable. It may make me judge him to be evil. But that I should be miserable, or that he should be evil, is irrelevant to my love.[13]

And in the concluding paragraph of the same section we read as follows:

We come, then, to the conclusion that love, as we see it in our present experience, involves a connection between the lover and the beloved which is of peculiar strength and intimacy, and which is stronger and more intimate than any other bond by which two selves can be joined. And we must hold, also, that whenever one of these selves is conscious of this unity, then he loves the other. And this is regardless of the qualities of the two persons, or of the other relations between them. The fact that the union is there, or that the sense of it is there, may depend on the qualities and relations of the two persons. But if there is the union and the sense of it, then there is love, whether the qualities and relations which determine it are known or unknown, vital or trivial. Qualities and relations can only prevent love by preventing the union, or the sense of it, and can only destroy love by destroying the union, or the sense of it. Love is for the person, and not for his qualities, nor is it for him in respect of his qualities. It is for him.[14]

On McTaggart's view, then, while approval—and, no doubt, disapproval—is always both because of and in respect of a quality—although it may be because of one quality and in respect of another quality—love, although it may be because of a quality, is never in respect of a quality. I must confess, however, that it does not seem to me that I approve of a quality, in the same sense that I approve of a man. A quality is, in my opinion, a universal which may characterize one or more particulars. If it be a member of that class of universals which we term values, we should, of course, respect or revere it; if it be a disvalue, we should condemn it. In either case, however, we simply recognize it for what it is. But if we believe in free will, our attitude toward the man whom it qualifies is very different. He could be other than he is, and we admire or despise him accordingly. In this sense, we should say a man is other than his qualities. If, however, McTaggart be right in his determinism, a man could not have had at any time other qualities than those he then possessed.

Now we can love, McTaggart tells us, because of some quality, or qualities. But this does not mean that our love is thereby rendered wholly explicable. For the quality, or qualities, possessed by C may, or may not, appear adequately to account for our love for C. "To love one person above all the world because her eyes are beautiful when she is young, is to be determined to vary great thing by a very small cause."[15] And in some cases no cause is discernible at all; in such cases, for instance, as are "recorded in *The Vita Nuova* and *In Memoriam.*"[16]

Whether determined by a very small cause or by no discoverable cause at all love, we are told, requires no justification for its presence. If it be genuine that suffices. Moreover, to whatever extent the beloved may be characterized by disvalues, this should not affect the devotion of the lover. Though it may do so, McTaggart admits, it ought not to do so. If the beloved be brutal, cruel, sadistic, selfish, dishonorable, stupid, and cowardly, love for him should remain unaffected by the recognition of this fact. "It seems to me," declares McTaggart, "that love towards a person known to be wicked is just as truly love (and, for that matter, just as good) as love towards a person known to be virtuous."[17]

Love, then, is an emotion felt toward a person and not toward his qualities. But does not this imply an absolute and inconceivable divorce between the person and his nature, if by his nature we mean the sum of his qualities? Would not an unqualified substance be disqualified as a metaphysical entity?

To love *because* of, one gathers, involves an indirect and inferential approach, whereas love in *respect* of involves direct and intuitive apprehension. But in either case, the love is for the person, not for the qualities. It may even be in spite of the qualities. In absolute reality, we are told, love will vastly outweigh evil; so it does not seem incredible that every self that is perceived will be loved. But in present experience evil qualities may, and often do, vastly outweigh the good.

In conclusion, then I must frankly confess that McTaggart's distinction between love *because* of and love in *respect* of qualities, on the one hand, and love for the person regardless of qualities, on the other hand, is to me unintelligible. But this does not weaken my conviction that his estimate of the place of love in the scale of values, and his view of its metaphysical significance, are profoundly true, and of the highest importance in the history of philosophy.

## NOTES

1. *The Nature of Existence*, vol. 2, sec. 463.
2. *Ibid.*, sec. 460. (I should prefer to say "a liking which is felt toward selves," inasmuch as it is possible for a man to love an animal, whereas it may be contended that only a rational self can be called a person. For McTaggart, however, in absolute reality all selves are persons.)
3. *Ibid.*, sec. 851.

4. *Philosophical Studies,* p. 266. Cf. *Studies in Hegelian Cosmology,* sec. 274.
5. *Ibid.,* sec. 465.
6. *Ibid.,* p. 144, n. 1.
7. *Loc. cit.*
8. *Ibid.,* sec. 465
9. *Loc. cit.*
10. *Loc. cit.*
11. *Ibid.,* sec. 466
12. *Ibid.,* sec. 467.
13. *Ibid.,* sec. 468.
14. *Ibid.,* sec. 468.
15. *Ibid.,* sec. 466.
16. *Ibid.,* sec. 461.
17. *Ibid.,* sec. 463

# IV

## *Mansel and Neo-Orthodoxy*

It is probable that relatively few philosophers or theologians today peruse the works of Dean Mansel. And yet they might do worse, for in his writings one finds much that is prophetic of the kind of thinking which is in vogue among the neo-orthodox, and one finds also the logical conclusions to which such thinking leads developed with a fearless lucidity which is as refreshing to the admirer of moral courage as it is appalling to one who has breathed the air of old-fashioned liberalism. In particular one discovers there the same conjunction of two currents of thought which is manifest in the work of such writers as Professors Kroner and Tillich. One current is that of the negative theology which, taking its rise in the Patristic period, later inundated the entire field of medieval speculation, and which, having penetrated various obstacles which once threatened to impede it, is again flowing with a newly acquired impetus. The other current is that which proceeds from the Kantian antinomies of pure reason. The blending of these two currents is due to a natural affiinity, the volume of one reinforcing that of the other. The negative theology assures us that the Divine Essence exceeds the grasp of human reason; the Kantian antinomies tell us why this is so—because of the inevitable and insurmountable contradictions in which human thought becomes involved when it seeks to transcend the limits imposed by sense experience.

It is a fundamental contention of Mansel—and one which he never wearies of repeating—that the Infinite and Absolute cannot be thought. Consciousness cannot exist without an object, and to

67

be conscious of an object involves a distinction between the object and what is other than it. But the Infinite cannot be thus distinguished from the finite; either by the absence of some quality which the finite possesses—for such a negative quality would constitute a limitation, and limitation is obviously incompatible with the notion of the Infinite—nor yet by a positive quality—for any quality of the Infinite will itself be infinite, and can be distinguished from the finite only by its lack of some quality which characterizes the finite, and such a lack will constitute a negative quality.[1] Again the Infinite cannot be identified with anything in particular, for then it would be subject to limitation, and would exclude all other particulars; hence, it must be actually nothing but potentially everything. On the other hand, since all potentialities must be realized in the Infinite, it must be actually everything.[2]

Furthermore, reluctant as the average Christian may be to acknowledge the fact, the Absolute cannot be conceived as conscious. For consciousness, as we have already seen, involves the relation of subject to object. Now that which is infinite and absolute can be confronted by no object external to itself. May it not, however, be its own object? Alas, this suggestion too is inadmissible.

> For the object of consciousness, whether a mode of the subject's existence or not, is either created in and by the act of consciousness, or has an existence independent of it. In the former case, the object depends upon the subject, and the subject alone is the true absolute. In the latter case, the subject depends upon the object, and the object alone is the true absolute. Or, if we attempt a third hypothesis, and maintain that each exists independently of the other, we have no absolute at all, but only a pair of relatives; for coexistence, whether in consciousness or not, is itself a relation.[3]

The Absolute, therefore, is incapable of functioning as a conscious and voluntary cause. But neither can it function as a necessary cause. For cause and effect are necessary to each other, and the Absolute can be relative neither to anything else nor to itself.[4] For the Absolute is neither a whole composed of parts, nor a substance composed of attributes; it is a unity transcending all relations.[5] For it to function as a cause it must be capable of becoming what it is not, which is self-evidently impossible. Thus the notion of creation in time is indefensible.[6]

Mansel reinforces these considerations by insisting upon the impossible consequences which follow from the assumption that the Absolute is a substance composed of qualities. The qualities of the Infinite, he repeats, must themselves be infinite. But, if the divine power be infinite, it cannot be limited by the divine goodness; nor can the divine justice be limited by the divine mercy; nor yet the divine foreknowledge by the divine freedom.[7]

From all this Mansel concludes that the Infinite and Absolute cannot be conceived as either this or that, as conscious or as unconscious, as simple or complex, as distinct from the universe or as identical with it—in short, that it cannot be thought of at all. Are we not, then, justified in asserting that what cannot be thought cannot exist, that the words *infinite* and *absolute* are mere *flatus vocis* which apply to nothing? Not at all, answers Mansel. The limitations of human thought must not be confounded with the limitations of reality. The existence of the limited implies the existence of the unlimited; hence, although we cannot conceive of the Infinite and Absolute, we are nevertheless constrained to admit that the Infinite and Absolute exist. But, to assert that what we cannot think of can yet exist, is equivalent to asserting that we can think of what we cannot think of—in other words, flatly to deny what at the same time we affirm.

Upon this resounding self-contradiction Mansel's entire system reposes. Yet it is nonetheless instructive to examine the course of thinking which has led him thus to stultify himself. It was obviously inspired by a Kantian subjectivism, and by the Kantian doctrine of the thing-in-itself. And this brings to light the curious fact that the Kantian thing-in-itself is only the philosophic counterpart of the theological entity which is the God of Maimonides—a God with respect to whom no positive statement can be made and to whom only negative qualities can be ascribed. That this Deity is also the God of the Barthians is

made clear by their repudiation of the *analogia entis*. And he—
or should I say it—is also identical with the God of Kroner who
can be approached only by religious imagination only after
reason has involved itself in insoluble contradictions, and with
the God of Tillich who—as he has informed us—is Being itself,
or the Absolute, and concerning whom "nothing else can be said
which is not symbolic."[8]

In justice to Mansel, however, it should be recognized that
he is by no means prepared to accept without qualification the
Maimonidean doctrine in all its stark negativity. Like the vast
majority of Christian thinkers he finds it necessary to supplement
the *via remotionis* by the *via eminentiae*. It is not enough to
assert that when God's anger is spoken of, what is meant is that
in distributing punishments, God *acts* like a man in wrath; nor,
when his love is referred to, that in bestowing benefits, he *acts*
as would a benevolent man. Mansel acutely observes:

> The conception of a God who acts is at least as human as
> that of a God who feels; and though both are but imperfect
> representations of the Infinite under finite images, yet while
> both rest upon the same authority of Scripture, it is surely go-
> ing beyond the limits of a just reserve in speaking of divine
> mysteries, to assume that one merely the symbol, and the other
> the interpretation. It is surely more reasonable, as well as more
> reverent, to believe that these partial representations of the
> Divine Consciousness, though, as finite, they are unable spec-
> ulatively to represent the Absolute Nature of God, have yet
> each of them a regulative purpose to fulfill in training the mind
> of man: that there is a religious influence to be imparted to us
> by the thought of God's Anger, no less than by that of His
> Punishments; by the thought of His Love, no less than by that
> of His Benefits; that both, inadequate and human as they are,
> yet dimly indicate some corresponding reality in the Divine
> Nature; and that to merge one in the other is not to gain a
> purer representation God as He is, but only to mutilate that
> under which He has been pleased to reveal Himself.[9]

The notion of a "regulative purpose"—obviously of a Kantian
derivation—referred to in the above passage is the key to Mansel's theory of analogy. Revelation, Mansel assures us, is not

*presentative,* but *representative.* A presentative knowledge of God would involve a capacity on the part of the finite to grasp the Infinite—a view which he believes himself to have shown to be self-contradictory. Moreover, were such the case, the competence of human reason would render revelation superfluous. And, in addition, such a view would imply that divine attributes differ from human, not in kind, but merely in degree[10]—a supposition which is clearly inconsistent with the doctrine of analogy. Revelation, then, must be representative. And what does it represent? What it represents must be "some fact of religious intuition." Indeed there are two such facts—the "feeling of dependence" and the "conviction of moral obligation."[11] In the recognition of the former we detect the influence of Schleiermacher, in the latter that of Kant.

Schleiermacher, however, was in error in believing that the feeling of dependence is revelatory of the nature of the Deity— and this for several reasons. In the first place, no inference can be drawn from it as to the moral character of the Power upon which man depends; it might just as well be evil as good.[12] In the second place, the greater the dependence, the less initiative will be found in the dependent; hence, complete dependence will involve complete intellectual incapacity to grasp the nature of that upon which one depends; the relation, in short, will be shrouded in a vagueness which will deprive it of all religious value.[13] In the third place, such a relation would be incompatible with the existence of human consciousness. "We can be conscious of a state of mind as such, only by attending to it; and attention is in all cases a mode of our active energy. Thus the state of absolute dependence, supposing it to exist at all, could not be distinguished from other states; and, as all consciousness is distinction, it could not, by any mode of consciousness, be known to exist.[14]

In the fourth place, prayer, which is an undoubted duty, involves an active relationship to God which is plainly incompatible with an absolute dependence which would be destructive of human personality.[15] And, in the fifth place, such absolute dependence would be incompatible with the fact of moral obligation. "If man's dependence on God," writes Mansel, "is not really destructive of his personal freedom, the religious consciousness, in denying that freedom, is a false consciousness. If, on the contrary, man is in reality passively dependent upon God, the consciousness of moral responsibility, which bears witness to his free agency, is a lying witness. Actually, in the sight of God, we are either totally dependent, or, partially at least, free. And as this condition must always be the same, whether we are conscious of it or not, it follows, that, in proportion as one of these modes of consciousness reveals to us the truth, the other must be regarded as testifying to a falsehood.[16]

From these contradictions Mansel can discover no escape.

When we turn to the fact of moral obligation similar contradictions confront us. Let Mansel state the situation as he sees it.

The moral consciousness of man, as subject to law, is by that subjection, both limited and related, and hence it cannot in itself be regarded as a representation of the Infinite. Nor yet can such a representation be furnished by the other term of the relation, that of the Moral Lawgiver, by whom human obligation is enacted. For, in the first place, such a Lawgiver must be conceived as a Person, and the only human conception of Personality is that of limitation. In the second place, the moral consciousness of such a Lawgiver can only be conceived under the form of a variety of attributes, and different attributes are, by that very diversity, conceived as finite. Nay, the very conception of a moral nature is itself the conception of a limit; for morality is compliance with a law; and a law, whether imposed from within or from without, can only be conceived to operate by limiting the range of possible actions.[17]

In truth Kant has been guilty of a stupendous inconsistency in attempting to conceive of the moral law as absolute, and as binding upon all rational consciousness which may exist, human or nonhuman. In so doing he has undertaken the impossible task of freeing himself from the essential limitations of human thought, of passing beyond the relative to the Absolute.[18] The only valid conclusion, Mansel contends, is that the unavoidable contradictions in which we find ourselves involved compel us to posit an Infinite and Absolute which *must* exist, but which cannot be thought. The medieval thinkers were right in maintaining that we can know *that* God is, but not what God is. And the proper function of the principle of analogy is to reveal to us not what God is, but *how* he wills us to think of him.

"We cannot say," declares Mansel, "that our conception of the Divine Nature exactly resembles that Nature in its absolute existence; for we know not what the absolute existence is. But, for the same reason, we are equally unable to say that it does not resemble; for, if we know not the Absolute and Infinite at all, we cannot say how far it is or is not capable of likeness or unlikeness to the Relative and Finite. We must remain content with the belief that we have that knowledge of God which is best adapted to our wants and training. How far that knowledge represents God as he is, we know not, and we have no need to know."[19]

That this way of thinking is utterly self-destructive, in that it requires us to think of the Absolute as, admittedly, we cannot think of it, I have already urged. The logical consequence of a Kantian subjectivism is a total agnosticism from which not even revelation could deliver us. What I wish to do now, however, is to call attention to the significance of Mansel's conclusions in the light of contemporary neo-orthodoxy.

When the neo-orthodox movement began it displayed a prudent unwillingness to oppose the then predominant liberalism all along the line. Thus it pointedly abstained from challenging the conclusions of Biblical criticism. And even today when it has gathered strength, although we hear a great deal about the fall of man and its disastrous consequences for human reason, about the unique status of Christianity, the absolute otherness of God, and the illegitimacy of the *analogia entis,* we do not hear a great deal about those doctrines which the liberal has always held in the greatest abhorrence—everlasting punishment, and the damnation of all non-Christians. The liberals' most eloquent protest against orthodoxy has been made upon moral grounds, and even the most reactionary theorists of today still find that protest impressive. Now it is one of Mansel's merits to have shown that, if one accept his fundamental contentions—which are so nearly identical with those of neo-orthodoxy—any such protest is wholly illegitimate. God is no doubt good, but since the divine goodness is other than human goodness and is totally incomprehensible, the fact that God is good can furnish no basis for inference as to what God may or may not do, or as to what he may or may not command man to do.

> That there is an Absolute Morality based upon, or rather identical with, the Eternal Nature of God, is indeed a conviction forced upon us by the same evidence as that on which we believe that God exists at all. But *what* that Absolute Morality is, we are as unable to fix in any human conception, as we are to define the attributes of the same Divine Nature. To human conception it seems impossible that Absolute Morality should be manifested in the form of a *law of obligation;* for such a law implies relation and subjection to the authority of a lawgiver. And as all human morality is manifested in this form, the conclusion seems unavoidable, that human morality, even in its highest elevation, is not identical with, nor adequate to measure, the Absolute Morality of God.[20]

As man is a man, and not God, so human morality is human and not divine. It is, indeed, *a priori* in the sense that it is psychologically ultimate, being rooted in the very constitution of the human mind. For, as Mansel says,

> to suppose that a moral law can be reversed or suspended in relation to *myself;* to suppose a conviction of *right* unaccompanied by an obligation to act, or a conviction of *wrong* unaccompanied by an obligation to forbear, is to suppose a reversal of the conditions of my personal existence; a supposition which annihilates itself; since those conditions are implied in the attempt to conceive of my personal existence at all. The Moral Sense is thus, like the intuitions of Time and Space, an *a priori* law of the human mind, not determined by experience as it is, but determining beforehand what experience ought to be. But it is not thereby elevated above the conditions of human intelligence; and the attempt so to elevate it is especially inadmissible in that philosophy which resolves Time and Space into forms of human consciousness, and limits their operation to the field of the phenomena and the relative.[21]

The consciousness of Time is connected with the science of numbers; that of space with the science of magnitudes; that of personality with the science of morals. But the very fact that moral obligations are imposed as divine commands indicates that although absolute in the sense that they are nonempirical and unalterable, they are yet relative to the peculiar status of man in the universe. Thus the prohibitions of murder, adultery, and theft in the Decalogue are plainly relative to beings possessed of physical bodies and endowed with material goods.[22]

If all this be granted it is evident that Mansel's conclusion is as inevitable as it is momentous; namely, that

> the primary and direct inquiry which human reason is entitled to make concerning a professed revelation is, How far does it tend to promote or to hinder the moral discipline of man? It is but a secondary and indirect question, and one very liable to mislead, to ask how far it is compatible with the Infinite Goodness of God.
>
> Thus, for example, it is one thing to condemn a religion on account of the habitual observance of licentious or inhuman rites of worship, and another to pronounce judgment on isolated acts, historically recorded as having been done by divine command, but not perpetuated in precepts for the imitation of posterity. The former are condemned for their regulative character, as contributing to the perpetual corruption of mankind; the latter are condemned on speculative grounds, as inconsistent with our preconceived notions of the character of God.[23]

Since we are entitled to no such "preconceived notions," condemnations of the latter sort are clearly out of order. Thus, to assert that a good God could not have required of Abraham the sacrifice of firstborn son, or have commanded Joshua to exterminate the Canaanites, would be as fatuous as it would be presumptuous. Hence what the liberal has taken to constitute genuine moral development of the highest order in our thought of God will be, if Mansel be right, in reality nothing but delusion. And it is difficult to see how the neo-orthodox avoid committing themselves to the same position.

This brings us to our concluding consideration, and one of

very great importance. The theistic hypothesis is an attempt to conceive of the universe as the expression of a conscious purpose which is both rational and righteous; it is an assertion of the ultimate reality and cosmological supremacy of Mind. Now we are acquainted with mind and purpose, with rationality and righteousness, only through introspection; however imperfectly we may exemplify these characteristics, it is to our experience as self-conscious beings that we owe our consciousness of them. Hence the theistic hypothesis depends for its intelligibility upon the possibility of ascribing these same characteristics *in the same sense* to ultimate reality; it reposes, in other words, upon the possibility of *univocal predication*.

The thinker who has grasped this truth most clearly, and has expressed it most forcefully, is Channing.[24] And liberal theology has in general proceeded, sometimes courageously, sometimes timidly, yet nonetheless inevitably, along the lines which he so prophetically forecast. Both traditional orthodoxy and contemporary neo-orthodoxy, however, are unwilling to enter upon this path. No sooner do they enunciate the theistic hypothesis than they begin to warn us that the divine consciousness is different not merely in degree, but in kind, from human consciousness, divine goodness from human goodness, divine wisdom from human wisdom, and so forth. In a word, they take away with one hand what they have given us with the other. Orthodox and neo-orthodox theism is halfhearted, inconsistent, and self-contradictory; is it not fair to say that it is not genuine theism at all?

That it is just to assert as much of neo-orthodoxy would seem to be rendered inescapably obvious by the blatant repudiation by neo-orthodox theologians of the *analogia entis*. Traditional orthodoxy, indeed, Calvinistic as well as Romanist, has befogged the issue by elaborating a doctrine of *analogous* predication. Yet is it not painfully clear, if the divine goodness and mercy, though "higher," are also different in kind from human goodness and mercy, that we simply have no idea as to what they are, and that, as Mansel has so cogently argued, we can draw no inferences from them, that Channing's emphatic statement of the case is wholly to the point. "We know not and we cannot conceive of any other justice or goodness than we learn from our own nature; and if God have not these, He is altogether unknown to us as a moral being; He offers nothing for esteem and love to rest upon; the objection of the infidel is just, that worship is wasted: 'we worship we know not what.' "[25]

The reason for this attitude on the part of the orthodox is obvious, for, as Channing so clearly saw, the admission of univocal predication leads straight to Unitarianism. For, if personality mean the same thing in God that it does in man, we cannot admit the reality of three divine persons without having three gods. But the inevitability of this consequence does not alter the fact that the theistic position is wholly dependent upon the possibility of univocal predication. Reject it, and Mansel opens his arms to you. Reject it, and behold a view which, while it may attempt to masquerade as theism, is in reality, when subjected to logical criticism, as nontheistic as any philosophy that has ever been elaborated.

## NOTES

1. *The Limits of Religious Thought,* pp. 93-94.
2. *Ibid.,* p. 94.
3. *Ibid.,* p. 78
4. *Ibid.,* p. 77
5. *Ibid.,* p. 78.
6. *Ibid.,* p. 77
7. *Ibid.,* pp. 78-79
8. *Systematic Theology,* p. 239.
9. Mansel, *The Limits of Religious Thought,* p. 223.
10. *Ibid.,* p. 71
11. *Ibid.,* p. 119.
12. *Ibid.,* pp. 120-21.
13. *Ibid.,* pp. 124-25.
14. *Ibid.,* p. 125.
15. *Ibid.,* pp. 125-26

16. *Ibid.*, p. 126
17. *Ibid.*, pp. 126-27
18. *Ibid.*, pp. 182-84.
19. *Ibid.*, p. 145
20. *Ibid.*, p. 186
21. *Ibid.*, pp. 185-86
22. *Ibid.*, pp. 187-88.
23. *Ibid.*, p. 210
24. See his sermon, "Likeness to God" and his famous review entitled "The Moral Argument against Calvinism."
25. *Works*, p. 464.

# V

## *The Perspective of Ontologism*

That the movement known to Roman Catholic theologians and philosophers as Ontologism should have been condemned merely as a heterodoxy, and not dignified by being classified as a heresy, doubtless accounts for the fact that it has attracted so little interest outside the denomination which in 1861 formally condemned it. Yet the idea which inspired it, when attention is once directed upon it, cannot fail to arouse keen interest in all who are concerned with the philosophy of religion. For its fundamental contention is that every human being is naturally endowed with a direct and intuitive knowledge of God. This is, indeed, a soul stirring claim. The awareness thus posited is declared to be both direct and confused, a description which will arouse familiar echoes in the ears of disciples of Leibnitz. Its origin, of course, is to be found in the philosophy of Plato, and the most eminent of its more recent expositors is none other than Malebranche. That it should have been welcomed by all theists would seem at first glance to have been a plausible supposition, yet the fear and hostility which it aroused were sufficient, as I have just said, to bring about its official condemnation. But before we consider the grounds for this decision, we should do well to review the chief forms in which it manifested itself.

We must, accordingly, distinguish between *Ontologismus Rigidus, Ontologismus Mitigatus,* and *Ontologismus Idealista.* In its first and extreme form Ontologism maintained that not only all universals, but also all forms of particulars are contemplated by the human mind as they subsist in the divine consciousness. Such was the position of Malebranche, and we can well

understand why it should have awakened the intense interest of
Berkeley, for Malebranche's assertion that we know of the existence of a material world only through revelation clearly indicates
how relatively slight was the difference between the viewpoints
of these two eminent thinkers.

In its second and more moderate form, Ontologism conceded
that physical objects are known in sense-experience, yet contended that general ideas or universals are known not by abstrac-
tion from particulars, but by intuition as they subsist in the mind
of God. The kinship of this view with Neoplatonism is, of course,
quite obvious.

*Ontologimus Idealista* is identified with the position of Ros-
mini, who maintained that all knowledge depends upon an intuitive awareness of ideal and indeterminate being as distinct from
real being. If I understand the theory aright this means being as
a universal apart from its concrete existence in God or in finite
particulars.

Outside Roman Catholic circles the most eminent expositor
of Ontologism, so far as I am aware, was the late William Ernest
Hocking,[1] but Father Pedro Descoqs,[2] who has discussed the
whole subject in detail, cites Husserl, Scheler, and Heidegger as
advocates in various ways of the same general point of view.

What is there, in Ontologism, we may ask, to account for the
intense opposition which it awakened in Neoscholastic circles?
Well, in the first place, in Christian theology the vision of God
is man's last end. It is the portion of the saints *in patria.* Hence,
if all men be endowed by nature with an intuitive awareness of
God, does it not follow that all men are now in Heaven? So
absurd a claim would certainly not be advanced by any sane
thinker. Moreover, if God be a Trinity, will not the three Persons
of the Trinity be objects of this awareness? How, then, are we
to account for the existence of Unitarians, Jews, Samaritans, and
Muhammadans, who presumably share this awareness? Again,
if all men be naturally endowed with a direct and intuitive awareness of God, must not all men be conscious of this awareness?
Must they not know that they know God? But, if so, how are we
to account for scepticism and atheism, or even for polytheism?

Cannot the ontologist successfully defend himself against these attacks by pointing out that the distinction between direct and indirect awareness must not be confused with the distinction between clear and confused awareness, and by emphasizing the confusion in our direct awareness of God, can he not render his position at least plausible? Indeed, if the awareness in question be confused enough, may it not give rise to almost any erroneous conception? Alas, the ontologist will still be open to attack from three different directions.

In the first place, it may be contended that a thoroughly confused apprehension is no better than no apprehension at all. If we do not know *what* we know, how do we know *that* we know? On the other hand, if we do know what we know, how is it that we are not in Heaven, and are not consciously in contact with the three Persons of the Trinity?

In the second place, we must remember that the God of the Scholastics and the Neoscholastics is a Being who is wholly simple. But, if a simple Being be known directly, must he not be wholly and clearly known? How, then, can it be maintained that the natural awareness of God possessed by all men is inferior to the vision of the saints *in patria?*

And, in the third place, if it be conceded that such direct knowledge of God as is possessed in this life by all men may in some be only potential, and not actual, how is the actual knowledge possessed by some to be distinguished from knowledge imparted by grace and not pertaining to nature? And will not any confusion of these two forms of awareness be disastrous for the philosophy of mysticism?

It must be admitted, I feel sure, that these objections retain their full force only in the perspective of Scholasticism. It is, perhaps, the second objection which at first sight seems the most formidable of all. How can a simple being be known at all, and not wholly and clearly known? Yet no less an authority than Saint Thomas has definitely asserted[3] that even among the saints *in patria* who perceive the divine essence in the light of glory one soul may perceive God more perfectly than another, and he uses the analogy of the greater and lesser degrees of warmth and coldness possessed by various entities in accordance with their nearness to or distance from a fire. Without attempting to criticise Aquinas's statement, I may point out that it might well be taken as proferring some comfort to the ontologist. Of course to most thinkers who do not adhere to the Scholastic tradition the notion of a conscious being in whom there is no distinction between quality and quality or quality and substance will seem quite unacceptable. Is not absolute simplicity, they will ask, absolute nonsense?

With regard to the first of these objections I can only submit that to me directness of perception does not seem incompatible with a considerable amount of confusion in perception. With how much? Who can hope to specify? In the face of criticism the ontologist found it advisable to lay stress upon this compatibility; at last Jules Fabre D'Envieu went so far as to expressly formulate a distinction between the *essence intime* and the *essence extime*, the former pertaining to the Deity in himself, and the latter to the Deity as related to creatures. In like manner D'Envieu drew a further distinction between two modes of apprehension—intuition and extuition—and, in accordance with this distinction, asserted that the *essence intime* is *intuited* by the saints *in patria* whereas the *essence extime* is *extuited* by human beings.

With respect to the third criticism we must admit that it is important for the Scholastic to distinguish between knowledge which pertains to human nature and knowledge which is the gift of grace. Natural knowledge is, of course, the property of all men, at least of all normal human beings. Hence the objection that if all men possess such knowledge all men must know that they do so would seem to be a very telling one. Yet cannot something be done with the distinction between potential and actual knowledge? May it not be the case that every man is by nature endowed with a potential intuitive awareness of God which requires effort to be rendered actual, with the consequence that actual awareness of God is the property only of some men?

In this connection we may take notice of the admission, which seems to constitute the extreme concession of the orthodox critic, that there may be a natural, direct, and confused awareness of God common to all men which can, however, be evaluated aright and known for what it is only in the light of formal and complete proofs of the existence of God supplied by metaphysics and based upon sense experience. To this view I shall return.

I have now said enough, I presume, with respect to the general issue as envisaged in Roman Catholic circles. It is obviously one of the first importance for all theists. But before I proceed to wider considerations, I think it advisable to compare and contrast the position of the ontologist with that of the Calvinist, for the two have much in common and yet are sundered by important differences. As seen by Neoscholastic eyes, Calvinism, of course, is no piffling heterodoxy; it is a full-fledged heresy. Yet at first glance, it might seem more opposed to Ontologism even than to Thomism, inasmuch as it roundly denies that there is any natural knowledge of God. All knowledge of God, it affirms, is a gift of grace—of common grace which is extended to all psychologically normal human beings and which leaves them without excuse, or of special grace which is extended only to the elect. But if man be a creature of God, he will owe to God all that he has. How, then, can a distinction meaningfully be drawn in what pertains to all men between what is of nature and what is of grace? The issue with respect to natural knowledge and common grace appears to have become a purely verbal one, yet I think that we may conclude that the ontologist has stated more intelligibly a view that is really common to both.

There is, however, a further issue. The ontologist has no objection to the philosopher's attempt to demonstrate the existence of God, for intuition and inferential knowledge, he holds, can mutually support one another. But the most distinguished recent expositor of Calvinism, M. Lecerf, asserts that all that a metaphysical argument can do is to show that if the universe can be envisaged as intelligible, the existence of a God must be posited.[4] Yet he has insisted this is not to prove the existence of the God of revelation, the "God of Jesus Christ." To this statement Professor Gilson has responded by pointing out that, if there be only one God, whoever has proved his existence has proved the existence of the God of revelation. Once more, it would seem, the Calvinist has been "hoist with his own petard."

I have not made this brief contrast between the positions of the ontologist and the Calvinist with the intent to adjudicate between them, nor yet with the intent to disparage Calvinism. The real greatness of Calvinism, as we find it in Jonathon Edwards, lies, in my opinion, in its insistence that the true approach to God is esthetic. But what I do want to emphasize is their common conviction that man is endowed with a direct, intuitive knowledge of God, a contention which is of importance to every religious man whatever be the sect or faith to which he adheres. However much importance we attribute to philosophical arguments for the existence of God, we must admit no argument has convinced everybody. It is also true, of course, that there is no argument which has not convinced somebody. And it may be plausibly urged that all the philosopher, as a philosopher, wants is to convince himself. But, as a human being, if he be thus convinced, he will wish that all men may share his conviction. Now if all men be endowed, whether by nature or by grace, with at least the potentiality of a direct, intuitive knowledge of God, may not the function of argument in this case be, as Professor Ewing has suggested, to clear the mind if its confusions and to focus its vision upon the divine existence?[5] Every valid argument reposes at last upon an insight that is ultimate; otherwise, the inferential process would go on forever.

Furthermore I would point out that for the kind of religious thinking which we call liberal, which owes allegiance to no historic doctrine and to no dogmatic authority, the hard and fast distinctions between nature and grace, between reason and revelation, between mystical and nonmystical awareness are now wearing thin. The Hegelians have familiarized us with a point of view which maintains that the more rational a religion, the higher is the degree of revelation which it exemplifies; and the more natural, the more clearly is it a product of grace. As far back as the anthropologist can trace the history of our race it has been a religious race. It is true that we know little or nothing about how religion originated; about that we can only speculate. Yet is it a plausible supposition that prehistoric men had to wait for prehistoric philosophers to awaken their religious interest? If our answer to this question be in the negative, are we not driven to posit some form of noninferential awareness?

Shall we, then, resort to the position of the ontologist? Should we decide to do so, we must be prepared to face a very embarrassing question. If the ontologist be right, ought not the most primitive manifestation of religion to have been some form of monotheism? Yet do not Hume's words ring true?

> We may as reasonably imagine that men inhabited palaces before huts and cottages, or studied geometry before agriculture; as assert that the Deity appeared to them a pure spirit, omniscient, omnipotent, and omnipresent, before he was apprehended to be a powerful, though limited being, with human passions and appetites, limbs and organs. The mind rises gradually from inferior to superior; By abstracting from what is imperfect, it forms an idea of perfection: And slowly distinguishing the nobler parts of its own frame from the grosser, it learns to transfer only the former, much elevated and refined, to its divinity. Nothing could disturb this natural progress of thought, but some obvious and invincible argument, which might immediately lead the mind into the pure principles of theism, and make it overleap, at one bound, the vast interval which is interposed between the human and the divine nature. But though I allow that the order and frame of the universe, when accurately examined, affords such an argument; yet I can never think, that this conclusion could have an influence on mankind, when they formed their first rude notions of religion.[6]

Convincing as these words sound, it may, perhaps, be contended that our confidence in them is misplaced. What of Father Wilhelm Schmidt's claim to have proved that monotheism was the primitive religion of mankind? Doubtless as a Roman Catholic theologian, Father Schmidt was pleased to advance an argument in favor of the traditional doctrine that the belief in God was communicated to our first parents by divine revelation, and that the subsequent history of religion consisted largely of a progressive forgetting of this primal illumination. But Father

Schmidt has insisted that his arguments are not philosophical nor theological, but scientific in character, and that if he is to be refuted, it must be done by an anthropologist. Let me assure you that I have no intention of encountering Father Schmidt on his own ground. I shall merely call attention to the fact that most anthropologists have not accepted his conclusion,[7] although they have admitted that he and Andrew Land have between them shown that the belief in a "high God" is far older than previously had been supposed. But this leaves the ultimate origin of religion still a matter of conjecture. Consequently, reinforced by this consideration, and supported, as I believe, by most investigators, I shall blithely revert to the position of Hume.

I propose, however, to emphasize two points on which, I believe, I can count upon a fairly wide agreement. The first is that inasmuch as polytheism, pantheism, and monotheism all have behind them an impressive background both of popular belief and of philosophic speculation, the direct awareness of the ontologist must be admitted to be very confused indeed. By saying this I do not presume dogmatically to discredit it. I mean only to maintain, as certain Neoscholastics, to whom I have referred, have maintained, that the ontologist's claim must be evaluated in the light of metaphysical arguments for the existence of God, and, I would add, in the light of the further study of mysticism which is so urgently a present need. In the second place, I would suggest that the worldwide prevalence of religion, its basic role in the development and progress of civilization, and its fundamental importance in human life are powerfully indicative of some direct, although confused, awareness of ultimate reality such as is posited by the ontologist.

Accordingly I make bold to advance an hypothesis of my own as worthy of consideration. It is one which doubtless may disquiet the theist, although I would plead that it ought not to do so above measure. My hypothesis is that every man is naturally endowed with a direct, although confused, awareness of his own underived and ultimate reality, that is, of his own eternity. This view, in my judgment, will go far to account for the universally entertained conception of the soul, which is the basis upon which religion everywhere is founded. Without the belief in the soul, the belief in gods and in a life hereafter would be inexplicable. The strength of this position, I submit, has been greatly reinforced by the definite rejection by contemporary anthropologists of the anamatistic hypothesis of a preanimistic stage of religious development.[8] Tylor's identification of animism with the initial stage now regains its original plausibility, and the objection that the plausibility is weakened insofar as it regards the origin of religion as dependent upon the speculations of primeval philosophers may be answered by the adoption of the hypothesis which I now propose. Without denying the possibility, or underestimating the role of primitive speculation, I maintain that, like all speculation, it presupposes an ultimate ground; that, like all inference, it rests upon direct intuition. I freely and willingly admit that my hypothesis must be evaluated in the light of metaphysical arguments which support it. Obviously I should transgress the limitations of the present paper were I now to undertake to enumerate and set forth such arguments, but I believe that they can be found and that they are conclusive.

## NOTES

1. See *The Meaning of God in Human Experience,* part 4.
2. See the *Praejectiones Theologiae Naturalis,* tomus primus, sectio tertia, capit. 1.
3. See the *Summa contra Gentiles,* liber tertius, capit. 58.
4. *Introduction à la Dogmatique Réformée,* second cahier, pp. 46-47.
5. See *The Fundamental Questions of Philosophy,* pp. 238-44.
6. *The Natural History of Religion,* sec. 1.
7. See Professor Mircea Eliade's *The Quest,* pp. 24-25.